Dressage
HOW TO...

HowToDressage.com

Copyright © 2020 by Rosanna Sunley T/A How To Dressage (HowToDressage.com)

All rights reserved

No part of this book may be reproduced in any form or by any electronic or mechanical means, including information storage and retrieval systems, without written prior notice from the author, except for the use of brief quotations in a book review.

Disclaimer of liability
The author(s) shall have neither liability or responsibility to any person or entity with respect to any loss or damage caused or alleged to be caused directly or indirectly by the information contained in this book. While the book is as accurate as the author(s) can make it, there may be omissions and inaccuracies.

ISBN: 9798664548051

Requests to publish work from this book should be sent to:
hello@howtodressage.com

RACEHORSE TO DRESSAGE HORSE

A SMALL NOTE...

There is no cookie-cutter approach when it comes to training horses. Every horse is an individual and must be treated as such.

This book makes informed, educated statements about thoroughbred ex-racehorses in general. However, not every horse will fit the same mold based on its previous training, temperament, and management.

We have done our very best to provide you with as much helpful information as possible, but you must be prepared to make your own judgment as to what is best for your horse and your unique situation.

If you are in any doubt, we recommend that you enlist the help of a trained and qualified professional who has experience in training thoroughbreds and rehabilitating ex-racehorses.

CONTENTS

| INTRODUCTION | 1 |

SECTION ONE – Introducing the racehorse	3
About the breed	4
Racing life	11
Reasons why racehorses are retired	19
After racing	22
Common myths	26
Why choose an ex-racer?	35

SECTION TWO – How to buy an ex-racehorse	39
Before you buy	40
Sourcing an ex-racer	45
Viewing an ex-racer	49

SECTION THREE – How to re-start an ex-racehorse	57
Step 1 – Letting down and health checks	58
Step 2 – Handling	67
Step 3 – Fitting tack	74
Step 4 – Lungeing and long-reining	88
Step 5 – Early ridden work	100

SECTION FOUR – How to train an ex-racehorse for dressage	115
The training scales	116
First schooling exercises	130
Fixing common problems	146
Schooling structure	177

SECTION FIVE – How to start competing in dressage	**189**
About dressage tests	190
Ex-racer only competitions	193
Competing against other breeds	197
First competitions	201
20 tips to improve your dressage scores	207
Using your scoresheets to improve	215
When to move up to the next level	221
BONUS SECTION – Jumping	**225**
How to start jumping your ex-racehorse	226
WHAT NEXT?	**233**

INTRODUCTION

Ex-racehorses often come with a bad reputation of being crazy and dangerous, as well as having a long list of health problems. The racing diet, lifestyle, and intense training push these horses to their limits both physically and mentally. No other equine sport demands so much from a horse, especially at such a young age.

But if the thoroughbred racehorse is transitioned adequately into his new career with patience and understanding, these horses can be one of the most generous, kind, highly intelligent, and eager-to-please breeds that you can find.

We are not exaggerating when we say that these horses can turn their hoof to almost any discipline after they have retired from racing. Our specialty is dressage (the clue is in our name!), so that is what we are going to be focusing on in this book. But even if you have plans to showjump, event, show, or do anything else with your off-the-track thoroughbred, the training outlined in these pages will give you the tools that you need to form a solid training foundation on which you can build.

Our aim is for the retired racehorse to transition successfully and to thrive in their new lives, whatever the discipline. We want you to be able to enjoy the process and for you and your new horse to build a mutual partnership based on trust and respect that will last a lifetime.

It will take time and patience by the bucket-load but trust us when we say that your efforts will be worth it! Here's to the start of your journey and your future success!

How To Dressage xx

SECTION ONE:
INTRODUCING THE RACEHORSE

ABOUT THE BREED

There are very few breeds that can claim to have influenced modern equestrian sport as much as the thoroughbred. So influential is the thoroughbred that the breed has been used to enhance the athleticism and refinement of many other breeds, including Irish Draughts, European warmbloods, Morgans, American Quarter Horses, and many more.

You will see thoroughbreds in many different equestrian sectors, from eventing and polo to hunting, dressage, and showing. Their bravery, willingness to work and people-oriented nature all combine to make these equines excellent all-around riding horses.

Primarily, though, the thoroughbred is bred to be a racehorse, and the breed is most well-known for that.

The origins of the thoroughbred breed

The thoroughbred breed evolved in Britain during the 17th and 18th centuries when horse racing was popular.

The British had been breeding what was termed, "running horses" for some while, and it was King Henry VIII who founded the first royal racing stables.

The thoroughbred breed was founded from three Arabian stallions that were brought to Britain by gentlemen who wanted to breed better racehorses. These lightweight horses were bred with Britain's heavier native animals to produce progeny that were stronger and faster than their ancestors while retaining the great stamina of the Arabian breed.

Just like human athletes, some thoroughbreds are more suited to sprinting, having muscles that contain many "fast-twitch" fibers, which produce sudden bursts of energy. Others are bred to be long-distance athletes, having muscles that contain more "slow-twitch" fibers that are able to produce a sustained effort for a longer period of time.

The three stallions

Byerly Turk

The Byerly Turk was the first of the principle bloodlines and stood at stud in County Durham.

Darley Arabian

The Darley Arabian was purchased in Syria and was brought to the owner's home in East Yorkshire. The stallion was put to the mare Betty Leeds, and their progeny became the first great racehorse, Flying Childers.

The bloodline also produced the famous racehorse, Eclipse, who founded the second bloodline.

Godolphin Arabian

In 1728, Lord Godolphin of Cambridgeshire brought the Godolphin Arabian to England. That horse was grandsire to Matchem, who leads the third bloodline.

So, all modern thoroughbreds are descended from those three stallions in the male line, with 81% of thoroughbred genes being derived from just 31 original ancestors.

Interestingly, none of the thoroughbred line's founding fathers ever actually raced!

The General Stud Book

The General Stud Book was the first official register of horses and was established in 1791.

The GSB listed only horses that could be traced back to the Byerly Turk, the Darley Arabian, and the Godolphin Arabian, and to 43 "Royal" mares that were imported during the reign of James I.

Racing classics in Britain

Toward the end of the 18th century and into the 19th, horse racing increased dramatically in popularity, leading to the creation of the English "Classics," including the St. Ledger, the Derby, the Oaks, and the 2,000 Guineas.

In the 1830s, the first steeplechases were run, having been adopted as an idea from Ireland. The most famous steeplechase is the Aintree Grand National, which was first run in the late 19th century and continues to attract huge audiences from right around the world.

Horseracing in the United States

In the U.S., which is now the world's biggest thoroughbred producer, flat racing first became popular in 1868.

In the early 20th century, bookmaking was banned, effectively curbing the sport until it bounced back when pari-mutuel betting was legalized in 1908. At that time, the first thoroughbred celebrities appeared in the form of Man O'War and Seabiscuit.

Following WWII, horseracing hit a flat spot until the 1970s when a new generation of equine stars emerged, such as Seattle Slew, Secretariat, and Affirmed who won the Triple Crown – the Kentucky Derby, the Preakness, and the Belmont – all U.S. Grade One races that are held within one month of each other.

The worth of thoroughbred racehorses

Horseracing, more so than pretty much any other sport, is driven by the betting industry that generates billions of dollars in revenue every year.

In the U.S alone., it's estimated that the racing industry and its various satellite industries are worth around $34 billion.

Racing is televised across multiple satellite channels every day that race meetings take place, all year round, and gambling on the horses has moved from high street betting shops and on-course bookies' stands to a massive, multi-billion-dollar online business.

Careers outside of racing

In Britain, around 5,000 thoroughbred foals are produced every year, with the U.S. breeding roughly 20,000.

Of those horses, only a tiny fraction become successful winners on the racetrack. However, many of those racing rejects find a second career in a wide range of equestrian disciplines, notably polo and eventing, where thoroughbreds have the speed and endurance that lend themselves perfectly to these two sports.

Although thoroughbreds are not generally seen at the top of the sport in modern dressage and showjumping, their athleticism and intelligence make them well-suited to competing.

Even ex-racehorses that don't go on to switch competitive disciplines often still find a future as a family pet and happy hacker.

Thoroughbred conformation

Unlike many other breeds, there is no "breed standard" as such for the thoroughbred.

Thoroughbreds are bred for speed, rather than attempting to establish a specific phenotype. However, there are some characteristics that enable a horse to run fast, and those assets make the thoroughbred instantly recognizable.

Ranging in height from 15hh to 17hh, thoroughbred horses have a deep chest, lean body, long, flat muscles, powerful hindquarters, long hind legs, well-angled shoulders, and a refined, intelligent-looking head. The thoroughbred profile is straight, without the dish of their Arabian ancestors.

The thoroughbred horse is built for speed. The key to their ability to run fast is the long distance between the horse's hip and hock that provides the animal with maximum thrust when galloping, together with a large depth of girth that enables maximum lung expansion and provides plenty of heart room.

Congenital soundness problems

Although thoroughbred horses are built to be supreme athletes, there are a few incumbent health problems that frequently appear in the breed.

A racehorse's training and competitive track career often begin when they are under two years old. Throughout the horse's career, its body will be pushed to its limits, and while many do remain sound, plenty don't. So, potential owners should be alert to problems such as stress fractures, sacroiliac damage, bone chips, and bowed tendons.

Also, some congenital conditions are thought to be due to the high percentage of inbreeding that has taken place. Problems such as exercise-induced pulmonary hemorrhage (bleeding of the lungs) and small, fragile feet that tend to be flat with thin walls and soles are often blamed on inbreeding.

Thoroughbred racehorse colors

Racehorses are given seven different official colors, which are shown as an abbreviation on race cards at race meetings alongside runners' information.

Recognized colors include:

- Bay
- Grey
- Chestnut
- Brown
- Black
- White
- Roan

At the time of writing, there are no colored (paint) racehorses in training.

Flat racers versus jump racers

So, you can see that thoroughbreds come in different shapes and sizes, depending on their bloodlines.

Some thoroughbreds are more physically suited to flat racing and may never race over fences. Other horses may add hurdling to their racing repertoire later in their career.

Flat racehorses begin racing at just two years of age in juvenile races. A lot of these thoroughbreds retire by the age of four, although there are exceptions. Many of the most prestigious flat races are restricted to three-year-olds, although flat racers generally peak aged four or five.

Jump racehorses begin their career on the flat, often in "bumper" races that are run at jump race meetings. Once the horse reaches four years of age, he can progress to competing in hurdle races, potentially graduating to steeplechasing if he shows the necessary aptitude and scope. Jumps racers don't reach their prime until they reach the age of seven to ten years.

Many former jump racers put their experience and training to good use after their racing career is over, finding a second career as eventers or showjumpers.

The thoroughbred birthday

Every thoroughbred horse born in the same year is given the official birthday of 1st January.

This means that two-year-olds born in the early months of the year are more likely to be stronger and more mature than later foals, despite officially having the same birthday.

RACING LIFE

The beginning

Horses are naturally flight animals, so galloping upsides another horse or within a group of horses comes naturally to them. Humans have simply learned to harness the horse's instinctive behavior and turned it into a sport - horseracing.

Thoroughbred racehorses are sold as foals, yearlings, at a "Breeze Up" sale as two-year-olds, or at the Horses-in-Training sales. Sometimes, a breeder sends their horse directly into training if they think it has a good chance of having a successful career.

Once the horse arrives at the trainer's yard, he will begin taking his first steps into becoming a racehorse.

Breaking-in and riding away

Horses that are bred to race on the flat are broken-in when they're around 18 months of age. Prior to that, the horse will have been extremely well-handled. He will have worn a bridle and bit, been shod, worn rugs, and generally been examined and handled by a variety of people.

Different trainers have their own preferences as to how the breaking-in process is carried out, but they all have the same goal which is to make the horse race ready. The horse is only taught the skills that he needs for racing.

Most horses are started in a round pen. They are worked in long reins and/or lunged, and only when that stage is fully established will the horse be expected to accept a rider.

When the horse has been backed, he will be "ridden away." During that process, the fledgling racehorse will learn to ride out with other horses, usually in the company of an older, experienced "nanny." The horse will learn to canter upsides other horses in groups, and they will also be asked to trot in figures of eight and work away from the other horses.

Taking a break

Once the horse has been broken-in and ridden away, he will be given a break over the Christmas period, during which time he will continue to develop mentally and physically.

In January, the horse will officially be two years old. At that time, racehorses are trained quietly and allowed to come into themselves while learning how to gallop.

To ensure that the horse's muscles develop evenly, he will be exercised in walk, trot, and canter on both reins with longer stirrups than are used for race training.

Learning to race

After the initial breaking period is complete, very little time is spent in schooling the horse, with most of the emphasis being placed on speed and fittening work.

When a reasonable level of fitness has been achieved, the horse may visit the main gallops. Usually, racehorses hack to the gallops and back again on a loose rein with very little input from the rider. The horses go out in a "string" and are accustomed to following the horse in front.

The gallops sometimes rise in a gradual incline. That work helps to develop cardiovascular fitness and build muscle. Work begins in a steady canter, gradually increasing in speed until the horse is ready to begin "sharp work."

Sharp work involves "jumping off" and then "breezing" over two or three furlongs (roughly one-quarter mile). That teaches the horse to "jump and run," which is what he will be expected to do in a race.

Although racehorses will be trained in both directions, most of their intense work will have them running counter-clockwise (to the left) since this is the direction that he will run in a race. Therefore, most racehorses will have more developed muscle on their left side.

On the gallops, the rider picks up a contact with the horse's mouth, leans slightly forward, and stands in the stirrups. That tells the horse to move off in canter. The rider then "bridges" the reins to give him a secure hold and allows the horse to "lean" on the rider's hand. If the rider shortens the reins or changes his grip, the horse will take that as a sign to increase his speed.

That's why your ex-racer will grab the bridle and go faster when you pull on your reins and try to slow him down. He's not bolting with you; he's merely doing what he was trained to do!

The work is often carried out with another horse alongside the youngster to train him to "race," while also teaching the novice that he must settle and listen to his jockey, rather than merely galloping blindly with no control of pace.

The job of a racehorse is to win races, not to carry the rider. It is the jockey's job to set the horse up but also to stay out of his way as much as possible to allow the horse to do his job.

When the work is established and the young horse is almost ready to run, he will be taught to enter and jump out of the stalls. That's a vital part of the training process as many races are lost because of a poor start. Also, if the horse is disobedient on race day and refuses to enter the starting stalls, he will only be given limited chances to do so before he is not permitted to run.

If the horse is repeatedly difficult to load at race meetings, the trainer may receive a fine, and the horse could be banned from racing until he can demonstrate that he will enter the stalls without causing problems.

Life in a racing yard

Racehorses are pampered creatures, living in the equivalent of five-star athlete accommodation. Every aspect of their care, including their nutrition, is tailored to help them perform at their absolute best.

Horses are creatures of habit on thrive on routine. Therefore, the daily routine of a racing yard can suit horses very well.

Each horse usually has the same lad or lass to care for them. That's important as it allows the horse to form a bond with his handler and also enables the carer to learn the horse's individual personality and idiosyncrasies and helps them to spot anything that's out of the norm.

Typical racing yard daily routine

The running of a racing yard takes a small army of trainers, grooms, secretaries, vets, and farriers.

Every yard will have their own routine, which will differ based on the facilities that they have access to, but below will give you a rough guide of a day in the life of a racehorse.

<u>5:00am to 6:00am – The grooms arrive</u>

Some horses are given a hard feed, and others are given a light breakfast of hay if they are one of the first lot to head to the gallops.

The horses are checked over and mucking out begins.

6:00 am to 12 noon – Exercising horses

The morning consists of groups of horses heading to the gallops, going on the horse walker, and/or being hot walked. Each horse usually receives 1 to 1½ hours' exercise and the trainer oversees three or four strings of horses every day, sometimes more.

The distance the horse runs will depend on the type of racehorse that he is. As a rule of thumb, short distance workouts are given to the sprinters, and longer workouts are given to distance horses.

When the horse returns from exercise, he is handed over to his groom/hot walker to be washed and warmed down so the rider can quickly get on the next horse.

12:30 pm – Lunch time

Horses will receive their second feed and the staff may break for lunch.

1:30 pm to 5:30 pm – General yard tasks

The afternoon is time for grooming and visits from the vet, farrier, physiotherapist, etc.

Some horses will be turned out for the afternoon to wind down after their morning exercise.

5:30 pm – Put to bed

The horses are brough in from the field, skipped out, and double-checked for any inflammation or injuries that may have occurred during training or turnout.

The horses are then given their main evening feed.

9:00 pm – Late night checks

Horses are checked on one last time to make sure that they are comfortable and have enough water and hay. Some horses may also be given another feed.

Weekly exercise routine

During the peak of the racing season, the horses' weekly exercise routine consists of fast gallop work twice weekly and steady trotting and cantering for the remainder of the week. Sunday is usually a rest day or quiet day, depending on the race schedule that is planned for each horse.

In National Hunt jumps yards, the horses may be schooled over jumps once or twice a week, either loose or under saddle.

Diet and nutrition

One of the most important elements of a racehorse's training is his diet and nutrition.

Most racehorses receive three to four hard feeds each day consisting of a scientifically formulated, high-quality, racing diet. Feeds contain high levels of protein and starch balanced with minerals and vitamins to ensure that the horses can perform to their optimum.

Although fiber is essential in any horse's diet, it can be extremely difficult to persuade a fit horse in training to each sufficient amounts of fiber each day.

Even though many of them have access to ad-lib hay or haylage, after their high-energy grain feeds, most horses do not each much of it. Because of this many ex-racers are found to have EGUS (Equine Gastric Ulcer Syndrome), which is thought to be caused in part by a lack of fiber in the horse's diet. (More about EGUS on page 63)

On race day

On race day, the horses are unloaded as soon as they arrive at the course and are put into a racecourse stable. That's why many ex-racer owners find that, although a dream to load, their horse won't stand quietly for long periods on the horsebox or in the trailer once you get to your destination.

The horses usually arrive at the racecourse at least three hours before racing. During that time, the horse can relax in the racecourse stables and may be given some water and a small, high-fiber feed.

All food and water are removed at least one hour prior to the horse's race. At that time, the horse is taken to the "pre-parade" ring, where he is saddled up in the "saddling boxes." Once saddled and ready for action, the horse is taken to the main parade ring, where he will experience crowds of racegoers and other distractions, such as catering stands, a public address system, and even brass bands.

Despite being incredibly fit and ready to race, the horses are expected to remain calm so that they don't waste valuable energy that they will need in the race.

Once the jockeys are legged-up, the horses are taken out onto the track to canter down to the start. Once there, the field walks around in front of the starting stalls, and their tack and girths are checked.

When the loading up process begins, the horses are walked around to the rear of the stalls and are loaded in a set order by the stall's handers. Loading can be a tense time, so it is essential that the horses are kept as calm as possible.

When the race is over, the winner is usually taken into the "dope box" where urine samples are checked for the presence of any prohibited substances. The horses are washed off and walked around until they have stopped blowing and are dry. Time is allowed for the adrenaline levels in the horse's body to settle down so that the horse is completely relaxed before traveling home.

Winners and also-rans

Although training winners is what racing is all about, not every horse will make the grade. For most owners, winning any race with their horse is a fabulous achievement, especially if that race is at one of the big festivals. However, most racehorses don't win even one single race.

Flat race trainers only have a couple of years in which to see each horse achieve its full potential. The clock is ticking and any horses that have not shown the ability to win a race by the time they are three years old will most likely not be kept in training, simply because of the cost.

So, what happens to horses when their racing career is over?

REASONS WHY RACEHORSES ARE RETIRED

A horse's racing career may be over at any stage; as a foal, during training, during their racing career, or when they are retired from the track because they are too old to race.

Horses that leave racing prematurely are described as "wastage." The main reason for a horse being taken out of training is poor performance either from a lack of talent or desire to race. Other reasons include injury, illness, lack of financial backing or behavioral problems, such as point-blank refusing to enter the stalls.

Let's look at some of the most common reasons.

Reason #1 - Lack of talent and/or desire to race

Some horses simply don't have the talent or the competitive edge that is needed for racing.

In these cases, the horse is retired so that the owner and trainer can move on to other prospects.

Reason #2 - Injury

A horse that cannot race is of no value to the owners, but not all racehorses which have been retired due to injury are a case to be avoided.

The horse may have suffered an injury which required time off, but this injury may not result in a permanent issue. However, due to the age limits which are imposed in racing, the owner and trainer may have decided that there's not enough time left to get the horse sufficiently fit and back in a race. Hence, the horse is retired.

Reason #3 - Not able to withstand the stresses of racing

Sometimes, an experienced trainer will see that the horse is not going to hold up against the stresses and rigors of racing. So, the trainer advises to retire the horse before he suffers an injury. This saves both the horse and the money of the owner and allows them to move on to more promising prospects.

Racing is one of the most demanding equine sports. Even if the horse was retired for this reason, the horse will most likely still be suitable as a dressage horse (or any other discipline).

Reason #4 - Lack of financial backing

Getting a horse to the races is an expensive endeavor. Care fees, training fees, license fees, race fees; it all soon adds up. It is estimated that only 6% of horses win enough money to cover their expenses. Therefore, cashflow can easily become a problem if the owners are unable to keep paying for this expensive luxury.

Other reasons may simply include the owner(s) losing interest or a syndication breaking down.

If the horse is showing great potential as a racehorse, then he may be sold to another racing owner. Otherwise, he is retired.

Reason #5 - No longer financially viable

Most racehorses will never win a single race. And if they do win a race, it becomes harder to win the next race due to some of the conditions designed to make racing fairer for less experienced horses.

In other words, once a horse wins a race, they may have to move up a level. The more races they win, the harder it is to win another.

Eventually the horse will have to run in open company. At this point, it will be unlikely that the horse will be able to make enough money to support his training bills and is therefore sold on.

Reason #6 - Got to the end of their racing career

Some horses do have long and successful race careers and have simply reached the end of it. They are now ready to retire into a less demanding discipline.

Although these horses have indeed clocked up the miles, they have proven that they can handle the stress and pressures of racing and remain sound. Therefore, these horses should not be overlooked.

AFTER RACING

When you consider that most racehorses only have a career on the track of two to three years when their life expectancy can be up to 30 years, it's little surprise to learn that there are plenty of ex-racers looking for a new purpose in life.

These days, public expectation is high that former racehorses will receive the appropriate care in their post-racing lives, not least because they have been purpose-bred for an industry that is worth billions of dollars.

So, what happens to the thousands of horses that leave training every year?

Stud farms

The thoroughbred bloodstock industry is massive. The aim of the game is to produce premium quality racehorses by maintaining and improving bloodlines. To that end, thoroughbred mares are only be covered by stallions that are licensed and approved.

Stallions that are successful on the racetrack are often worth a small fortune in stud fees, even after their racing career has long finished. For example, the stud fee for the hugely successful sprinter, Frankel is reportedly around £125,000 (roughly $155,500) and he could cover over 100 mares per year.

Mares that are well-bred can also have a second career as broodmares, even if they did not have outstanding success on the track.

The thoroughbred breeding season runs from mid-February through June. Mares are brought from the mares-only "boarding stud" when they begin ovulating to the covering shed of the stud where the stallion is standing.

The breeding industry is extremely lucrative, and horses that are involved in it are treated exceptionally well. Although a few people might disagree, on the whole, life on a stud farm is not too shabby a retirement fate for a racehorse!

Slaughter

Sadly, some ex-racehorses are "put down."

In the UK, there are around 5,000 horses being retired from racing every year, and sometimes there is no option but to send these unfortunate animals to slaughter, as there simply isn't enough room to house them.

Some animal rights campaign groups believe that over-breeding of thoroughbreds is one reason for the mass culling that takes place each year, and the fact that many of those horses are aged five or under is a tragedy.

The luckier ones are humanely destroyed in a relatively peaceful manner, whereas others are dispatched by means of a bullet through the temple or a metal bolt into the side of the brain. The carcasses are then taken on refrigerated lorries across the English Channel to France where they are sold as meat.

What a desperately sad end to a once-cherished and pampered animal who simply didn't make the grade.

Is there a solution to the problem?

There are calls for the breeding program that exists within the racing industry to be curtailed, and around the world, racing authorities are attempting to help vulnerable horses, while a range of charities carry out sterling work too.

Re-training and re-homing

Many charities are working tirelessly to find new jobs and new homes for retired racehorses.

Thoroughbreds can lend themselves to many other activities outside of racing, including dressage, showing, polo, eventing, and show jumping. Also, there are plenty of thoroughbred ex-racers that cannot be ridden for various reasons, but they make wonderful companions for youngstock, and many are sound and suitable to be shown in-hand.

Obviously, some horses are better at some disciplines than others, just as people are. However, thoroughbreds are typically athletic, intelligent, durable, and keen enough to handle lots of different jobs away from the racetrack.

Taking on a former racehorse is an incredibly satisfying and rewarding thing to do, and you could be saving a life.

Most countries where horseracing is popular have a whole host of organizations that are dedicated to the re-training and rehoming of retired racehorses. Listed below are just a few of these well-known ex-racer charities:

TCA (Thoroughbred Charities of America) – www.tca.org

The TCA is an umbrella group whose website lists all the many racehorse rehoming charities right across the United States, together with contact details and further useful information.

RoR (Retraining of Racehorses) – www.ror.org.uk

The RoR is the BHA's official charity that supports ex-racers. The charity uses funds from within the racing industry to provide a safety net for vulnerable horses that have been retired from racing.

Supported by famous star jockeys, Frankie Dettori and Richard Johnson, the RoR prepares horses for a new career and matches them with suitable "foster" homes where they can enjoy a new lease of life.

Godolphin Rehoming Program – www.godolphinlifetimecare.com

Godolphin operates rehoming initiatives for their ex-racers in Europe, the US, Japan, and Australia.

The horses are given a short holiday before being retrained. Once the horse's strengths and aptitudes are established, the Godolphin team will find the lucky horse a suitable new home.

The British Thoroughbred Rehabilitation Center (BTRC) - www.britishtrc.co.uk

The BTRC was the first UK charity dedicated to the welfare of ex-racehorses. The charity takes horses straight from the track or from post-racing homes and looks to secure the future of those horses for the remainder of their lives.

HEROS (Homing Ex-Racehorses Organization Scheme) – www.heroscharity.org

HEROS is a well-established ex-racers homing scheme, which provides a home for racehorses when their career is over. The charity works to find homes that are suitable for each individual horse.

COMMON MYTHS

Unfortunately, ex-racehorses do have a pretty bad rep. After all, they can't be up to much, or they wouldn't be so cheap to buy right off the track, would they? And when have you ever seen an ex-racer winning a top-level dressage competition – they simply don't have the temperament or the paces, right?

In this part of our guide to buying and re-training an ex-racehorse, we take a closer look at some of the common myths that surround these beautiful creatures.

By the time you've finished reading this chapter, you'll have a much clearer idea of what's fact and what's simply misguided fiction when it comes to ex-racehorses.

Myth #1: Racehorses don't hack out

It's a common belief that racehorses do not hack out. Actually, they do. From an early age, many racers are long-reined around quiet lanes to get them used to different sights and sounds.

Once backed, racehorses hack out in "strings," first as part of a fittening program, and then to get to and from the gallops when they're in training.

Usually, the horses take it in turns to lead, after all, a racer that refuses to go to the front is neither use nor ornament on a racetrack!

Myth #2: Racehorses can't be turned out

Although most racehorses are not turned out 24/7 while they are in work, many do get a couple of hours' turn-out in a small paddock every day. So, when you take on an ex-racer, you will be able to turn him out, and he will know what a water trough is and how to use it!

However, do bear in mind that your new acquisition won't be accustomed to spending all day out in the elements, so do introduce all-day turn-out gradually, and be sure to kit your horse out in a suitable rug if the weather is cold or wet.

Also, thoroughbreds have sensitive skin, so make sure that your horse has adequate fly protection in the summertime, especially around his face.

Myth #3: Racehorses are not good doers

If your ex-racer has trouble maintaining condition or gaining weight, it's most likely due to a range of issues, including (but not limited to):

- Dental problems
- Gastric ulcers
- Worms
- Stress

These are all problems that can be resolved through correct management and providing the horse with an appropriate diet for the amount of work he is doing.

Myth #4: Thoroughbreds have bad feet

That myth is partly true.

Comparative to their size, racehorses are bred with relatively small feet. Also, their hoof walls and soles tend to be thinner.

The lifestyle and nutrition of a racehorse does not aid hoof heath and growth and when in training, he can be re-shod as little as every 3-weeks. So, it's no wonder that many new owners of OTTBs complain of bad feet and poor hoof quality.

However, with good nutrition, correct trimming and care, there's no reason why a thoroughbred shouldn't have good feet.

Remember that a horse fresh from the track will need time to adjust to wearing heavier shoes, rather than lightweight aluminum racing plates. If you wish to transition your horse to going barefoot, this can also be done providing it is suitable and comfortable for the horse.

Whatever route you choose, we recommend working with a good farrier and following their advice on how to manage your horse's feet to improve their condition and health.

Myth #5: Racehorses won't pick up their hind feet

Most racehorse wear a full set of aluminum plates and are shod more frequently than normal leisure horses, so they will pick up their hind feet when asked to, just like any other horse does.

It is worth nothing here that racehorses often have all four feet picked out from the left side of the horse. But don't worry, the horse will still be accustomed to the farrier working from the right side so this shouldn't pose an issue, it's more like a fun fact!

Myth #6: Racehorses can only go one way

Since 1921, all racecourses in the U.S. have run counter-clockwise, or lefthanded. In the U.K., most racecourses also run lefthanded. There are several that run clockwise or righthanded, and a few that run in a figure-eight layout.

Although your ex-racer will have been trained in both directions, it is likely that most of his intense work would have been on the left rein. This can cause the horse to develop more muscle on that side.

This doesn't mean that your horse is incapable of going on the right rein or cannot canter on the right lead. With correct and systematic schooling, the horse will be able to work on both reins equally.

Myth #7: Racehorses have stable vices

Some racehorses do have stable vices, just like many other breeds of horses!

However, racing yards have a strict routine, which suits most horses perfectly. All horses are more relaxed and happier when they have a routine, and they know when to expect food, company, exercise, etc.

Ideally, you should give your ex-racehorse a routine, too, including as much turn-out time as possible. When the horse is stabled, be sure to keep him entertained by providing plenty of forage, toys, adjacent company, and other distractions.

Due to their high-energy grain diets, some ex-racers may demonstrate stable vices when you first bring them home. But as they are "let down" and relax into their new and more leisurely lifestyle, these vices may disappear.

Myth #8: Ex-racers are crazy and strong!

Some ex-racehorses can be excitable and strong, but the same is true of any breed. In fact, racehorses are often taken out of training because they are too slow, too lazy, or simply not interested in galloping!

When a racehorse is in training, he is kept extremely fit and lean, and he's fed a diet that is designed to provide him with maximum energy. Understandably, racers can, therefore, be on the "hot" side, but even the calmest of horses would be highly spirited if fed this diet consistently.

With the correct adjustment to the horse's training, feeding, management, and plenty of relaxation time in the field, most ex-racers can be safe to ride and handle.

Myth #9: It's impossible to find a saddle to fit a racehorse

That myth stems from the fact that some ex-racers have high withers. However, that shouldn't be a problem for an experienced saddle fitter. They are not the only high-withered horse out there! (More about saddle-fitting on page 74)

Myth #10: Ex-racehorses are unsound

Many people assume that ex-racehorses come with soundness issues, and that's the reason they are no longer in training.

Obviously, racing can take a toll on horses' legs, but as we discovered earlier in this book, racehorses can be retired for many different reasons. The most common being that he is just too slow to justify the financial outlay for no return, in which case, the horse is retired sound.

That said, you should always have any horse vetted before you take it on, regardless of his history, breed, or age. This will flag any potential issues with regards to soundness.

Myth #11: Racehorses are naughty and hard to handle

Big racing yards are extremely busy places, so the horses simply have to be obedient and mannerly. Racehorse lads and lasses do not have time to waste with a fidgety horse that won't stand still to be groomed, washed down, shod, tacked-up, or clipped!

Also, ex-racers are almost all excellent loaders. They are accustomed to traveling to and from race meetings week in, week out, so most are good travelers too. Many former top flat racers will also be seasoned frequent flyers!

Remember that when in racing these horses are young, extremely fit, and fed a high-energy diet. When "let down" most of these horses are calm and obedient and display excellent manners.

Myth #12: Racehorses are pullers and have no brakes

Racehorses are taught to run into the bridle and to "take hold" of the bit.

It worth noting here that it is the horse that holds the bit, not the rider holding the horse.

If you watch a race on TV, as the horse begins to drift back through the field and lose momentum, you'll hear the commentator remark that the horse has "dropped the bridle."

It's really a matter of teaching the horse as part of the re-training process that a rein contact doesn't mean "go faster."

Thoroughbreds are usually intelligent and quick to learn, so the pulling habit is not generally an issue and can be cured relatively easily.

Myth #13: Racehorses' paces aren't good enough for dressage

Some people are disparaging about ex-racers, saying that they don't have good enough paces for dressage.

It's important to remember here that **dressage is for the horse, the horse is not for dressage.** Therefore, any horse can be successful in dressage, as long as his paces are correct and regular.

Racehorses are usually bred to have an exceptionally good walk, largely because if a horse walks well, he will be able to gallop well too, and a good walk is crucial for dressage horses.

Much can be done to improve a horse's balance and self-carriage, which in turn will help him make the best of his trot and canter.

Myth #14: Racehorses have tough mouths

Any horse can have a hard mouth, regardless of its breeding and history.

While it is true that racers are trained to run into the bridle, it's worth nothing that racehorses are almost always ridden in a soft snaffle-type bit, and with re-training and correct schooling you can re-educate the mouth and teach them to adopt a correct contact.

Myth #15: Racehorses cannot collect

Thoroughbreds often have a natural conformation that places them onto their forehand, which can make it a little difficult for them to work in collection.

However, systematic training will bring about the muscular development and strength that's necessary to enable a horse to take more weight onto the hindquarters, lifting the forehand, creating a more uphill balance, and allowing the rider to develop collection.

In a nutshell, if trained correctly, your OTTB will be able to show degrees of collection.

Myth #16: You cannot put your leg on a racehorse

When they are first backed, the exercise riders will have much longer stirrups to the short 'jockey length' stirrup which we see on TV. This helps with balance on a young horse that is starting to learn how to gallop.

The riders do not use their legs the same as a dressage rider, but they have had legs on them, and with time and patience you can re-school the racehorse to understanding new leg aids.

Myth #17: Racehorses will struggle with flying changes

Any breed of horse can struggle with learning how to perform a flying change, even a purpose-bred dressage horse!

However, racehorses are in fact taught how to change their leading leg early on in their training.

When racing, the horse will usually run on the left lead through the left turn. However, on the final straight, the jockey will sometimes ask the horse to change to the right lead by shifting their weight into their right stirrup.

So, an ex-racer will already know how to change their leading leg, you just need to remodel the aids and the balance.

Final verdict ...

As you can see, most of these perceived issues can be dealt with through the correct feeding, management, and training of the horse.

When taking on a retired racehorses directly from the track, you are not buying a finished product, so, undoubtedly, you have a lot of work to do when you decide to offer him a home and transform him into a dressage horse.

It will take time and patience, but your efforts will be rewarded many times over when you trot down the centerline for the very first time.

WHY CHOOSE AN EX-RACER?

Shopping for a horse is never an easy task, regardless of the breed or the job you want the horse to do.

However, there are a plenty of good reasons for choosing to rehome a former racehorse as your next dressage partner:

A full history

Unlike many homebred horses, every racehorse has a full pedigree that's easily researched. You can also check out the horse's race record, previous trainers, and former owners.

If the horse has raced, you can find footage of those races on several websites, including ATR (At The Races), Racing UK, ITV Racing, and others.

Often, you also get to see the race preliminaries, which will give you a fairly good idea of how the horse behaves in the stressful, exciting environment of the racecourse.

Proven soundness

Soundness is absolutely critical when it comes to buying a horse for dressage. Racehorses are checked on a daily basis for soundness and any problems are treated right away.

If the horse fails to perform as expected in a race, he will be examined straight away by the trainer's vet. Blood tests are usually taken, and the horse may undergo an endoscopy too.

Also, you can take a look at the horse's race record. Any long absences from the track can be indicative of soundness problems and should be investigated further.

If the horse has retired sound, then you know he has been able to withstand the intense pressure and stress of racing and this bodes well for his future career.

But as with any horse, you must have your ex-racer examined by a vet prior to purchase who will check for pre-existing injuries or conformational quirks that could predispose the horse to soundness issues in the future.

Been there and done it!

From the age of one, racehorses are consistently handled, and they start their ridden careers as two-year-olds. By the time the horse reaches its third year, it will have been ridden daily in the company of others, often hacking out in a string along quiet roads to reach the gallops.

Throughout their career, they would have had more than one rider and would have learned how focus on their job with lots of other horses and distractions going on around them.

They would have experienced regular grooming, bathing, tacking up, travelling, hacking, farriers, vets, physios, racing events, and more.

At this point, they have had much more life experiences compared to other breeds of a similar age.

Financial savings

Unfortunately, failed or retired racehorses are not considered to be of any great value. The general public often view ex-racers as unwanted, and other breeds have been marketed much more effectively.

Consequently, if you buy an ex-racer, there's a good chance that you'll get a bargain.

Also, you could choose to adopt an ex-racehorse from a charity. Although you'll need to make a donation to the organization, it will probably be less than the market value of the horse.

However, please do bear in mind that the cost of the initial purchase is only part of the equation. The ongoing care costs are not cheap and therefore the decision of buying a horse should not be taken lightly.

Ready to go

Not all ex-racers are completely green, and you don't need to purchase straight from the track.

If you choose to adopt a horse from an ex-racehorse rehabilitation charity, there's a good chance that the horse will be familiar with being ridden in an ordinary saddle, he will have an understanding of the basic aids, and will be ready to progress with his education.

Also, the re-training center will be able to tell you all about any particular quirks that the horse has, so you won't have any nasty surprises when you get him home.

The feel-good factor

After a thoroughbred's racing career has come to an end, his future can look very uncertain. By rehoming and re-training an ex-racehorse you are giving him a second chance and a new purpose. Not to mention that you may also be saving his life.

SECTION TWO:
HOW TO BUY AN EX-RACEHORSE

BEFORE YOU BUY

Before you jump in and buy an ex-racer, you need to be sure that a thoroughbred is the right choice of equine partner for you and your circumstances.

General things to consider before you go horse-shopping

Before you set out to search for your perfect equine, there are some questions that you must ask yourself. The answers to these questions will, to some extent, determine whether an ex-racer is the best choice of horse for you.

Question 1 - Do you want to loan, lease, or buy?

Sometimes, loaning or leasing a horse can be a good option, especially in times when job security is uncertain. If your circumstances change and you can no longer keep the horse, a loan or lease agreement means that you can return the horse to its owner, without the hassle of trying to sell it on.

Most racehorse rehoming charities insist that their horses are "adopted" rather than purchased. So, instead of buying the horse outright, the adopter makes a donation to the charity, and that money is put towards helping other unwanted ex-racers. If the adoption doesn't work out at any point in the future, you can return the horse to the charity.

Leasing a horse essentially means that you pay the owner a fee each month for the privilege of having the horse on a loan footing. So, although you won't need to pay a lump sum upfront for the horse, you will have to pay the lease premium each month on top of the horse's general running costs, and sometimes, a deposit is required at the commencement of the lease.

Question 2 - What's your budget?

First of all, you need to know exactly how much you have to spend on a horse upfront.

Too often, ex-racehorses are seen as a "cheap" option by people who are desperate to own a horse but have limited funds with which to buy one. Remember that, regardless of the horse's purchase price, the running costs will be pretty much the same. Which leads us into our next question...

Question 3 - Can you afford to keep the horse?

Keeping a horse is not a cheap undertaking!

The following are all extra costs that you will have to pay each month toward the horse's upkeep:

- Livery costs (if you don't have your own facilities)
- Feed, bedding, forage, etc.
- Insurance
- Farrier's costs
- Veterinary fees/vaccinations/worming etc.
- Equine dentist/physio/therapy
- Lessons and training
- Competition entry fees/society registration costs

Although you may be lucky and inherit some of the horse's tack and rugs as part of the purchase or loan agreement, you will most likely need to buy some new gear too.

You should also consider the horse's retirement. It's obvious that one day the horse will retire from all ridden work so it's best to plan for this ahead of time to ensure that the horse's future is secure.

Question 4 - Where are you going to keep the horse?

If you have your own yard or stables and paddocks, that can save you a lot of money and hassle.

Livery yards can be expensive, depending on what facilities they have to offer. There are almost always rules and regulations to abide by, which could make or break your enjoyment of your time with your new horse.

However, keeping a horse at home also requires that you upkeep your land, stabling, and arena if you have one. And all that costs time and money.

Here are some things you consider when deciding where to keep your horse.

- If you have a busy life and a full-time job, can you afford to pay for full livery for your horse?
- Do you have ready access to a riding arena, or do you have to travel to reach one?
- Does the arena have a good-quality surface that's well-maintained?
- Does your yard offer year-round turnout?
- Is there a horse walker that you could use on days when you can't ride?
- Are you hoping to keep your horse on a dressage yard? (Like-minded, enthusiastic individuals can make dealing with problems easier and sharing knowledge is invaluable.)

NOTE: If you're intending to keep the horse at livery, make sure there is a vacant stable on the yard of your choice **before** you begin looking for a horse.

Question 5 – Can you give the horse the time it needs?

When re-trained correctly, these horses will give you their everything, but this is not a quick turnaround. The process requires a lot of time and a lot of patience.

Please don't take on an ex-racehorse unless you are able and willing to give the horse all the time it needs to learn its new job.

Every horse is different, and this timeframe will vary greatly.

Question 6 – What do you want to do with the horse?

By choosing to purchase and read this book, I'm guessing that you would like to transition your OTTB into a dressage star.

However, should you want to do other activities, such as showjumping or eventing, then these need to be taken into considering when choosing your ideal equine partner.

This will also help to dictate what temperament and physical flaws you are willing to accept. For example, if you are planning to show the horse, then any blemishes are a big no.

Question 7 – At what stage of re-training would you like your ex-racehorse to be?

You can buy an ex-racehorse at various stages of re-training, and each stage comes with its own benefits and risks.

For example, you can buy straight from the tack. This is probably going to be your cheapest option, but it is also going to require the most work and carry the most risk.

Alternatively, you can buy a horse that has been retired from racing for several years. This is probably going to cost you a little bit more, but there will be less risk as you will be able to ride the horse and see how he handles life as a regular riding horse.

Answering this question will help to give you some idea of where to look when sourcing your future equine partner. Which leads us nicely into the next chapter of this book.

SOURCING AN EX-RACER

So, you've decided that an ex-racer is a suitable choice of horse for you. Your answer to Question 7 in the previous chapter will dictate where you should start looking to source a suitable horse.

Here are the options that are available to you.

Racehorse rehoming centers

Wherever you are in the world, there are many charities that have been set up to help rescue and rehome unwanted racehorses whose track career has come to an end. (Some are mentioned on page 24)

These centers are mostly run by people with many years of experience in handling and training ex-racers, and they make an excellent place to begin your search.

Set aside some time for an online search and spend it trawling through the websites of all the thoroughbred rehoming centers that you can find in your country and/or area.

All the main thoroughbred rehoming charities have websites where you can find listings of horses that are available for sale or adoption. Some include video footage of the horse being handled and ridden, as well as a gallery of photos and a potted history of the horse's pedigree and former career.

You'll be expected to make an initial email enquiry, or complete an application form, where you will be asked to provide details of your previous riding and horse-owning experience. Based on the information that you provide, the center will match you with prospective horses that you can go to see.

These charities are very experienced in handling ex-racers and understand their suitability for second careers. You will be able to watch the horse being ridden and ride him yourself, too, under supervision.

Most rehoming centers are looking for people to adopt or foster their horses rather than buy them outright. Although the centers are hopeful that the horse will find a forever home, the adopter always has the option to return the horse to the center if things don't work out or circumstances change.

You will be expected to pay an adoption fee to the center, and you will have to sign an adoption agreement that is designed to protect the horse in the future. The reason for that is two-fold.

Firstly, all these organizations are charities not retailers. So, by taking an adoption fee rather than selling the horse, they can avoid paying duty or tax on any money that they receive. That means that the donation can be used to take on and retrain more horses retiring from the track.

Secondly, the center can be confident that none of their horses will ever be resold to an uncertain future if things don't work out the first time around.

At the track or straight from the racing yard

If a trainer has a horse that is due to come out of racing in the near future, it may be possible for you to arrange to go and view the horse.

In some cases, you can watch the horse training at the yard or possibly watch it race. But you won't be allowed to ride the horse yourself unless you have a jockey's license.

Buying straight from the yard can be the cheapest option, but it can also be the riskiest since you won't know a great deal about what the horse's temperament will be like after he is "let down" and the trot-up won't show you much of the horse's natural movement.

Agents

There are people whose job it is to match horses and riders. Many of these agents are also riding instructors and trainers.

If you decide to go down this road, do check that the agent has experience in dealing with ex-racers and has good connections in the industry.

A good agent will review the online listings that you're considering, visit the horses with you, ask the vendor all the right questions, and save you the time and hassle of viewing horses that are unsuitable for you.

Some agents will charge you for their time, whereas others will charge a percentage of the purchase price of the horse.

Professional trainers and dealers

Some ex-racers are purchased direct from the track by experienced professional trainers and dealers. These people reschool the horses and sell them on when their value has increased.

Some trainers will take a horse and retrain it for the owner for a fee. Others may act as the owner's agent, re-training the horse, competing it so that its value increases, before selling it on.

Professional trainers can be an excellent resource for racing owners who want their horses to have a second career and a more certain future. Also, for anyone looking to buy an ex-racer, a dealer and trainer with a good reputation can be an excellent place to search for a horse.

Equine sales and auction markets

Although this route can initially appear to be a cost-effective option, you should only undertake buying a horse from a sale or auction market if you are very experienced and sales-savvy.

You don't get to see much of the horse, other than it being paraded around a small pen, and you often have little or no comeback if the horse you buy turns out to be unsuitable.

Also, you won't be able to have the horse thoroughly vetted if you buy through a horse sale, meaning that you could discover all kinds of soundness problems when you get your purchase home.

VIEWING AN EX-RACER

Buying a new horse is a very exciting time. However, it's important that you keep a cool clear head so that you don't rush into any decisions which you may regret later on down the line.

So, here is some helpful advice when it comes to viewing.

Who to take with you

When viewing a horse (any horse) it's advisable that you take along a knowledgeable person. Ideally someone who is familiar with your riding experience and capabilities, for example, your trainer.

It's very easy to get emotionally attached to a horse when viewing them, even though they might not be a suitable horse for you personally - we are all horse lovers at the end of the day!

What to look for

Thoroughbreds come in all different shapes, sizes, and colors. When choosing an ex-racehorse for the discipline of dressage, here are some qualities to look out for.

<u>Movement and paces</u>

It is particularly important for dressage that the horse has 3 correct paces:

- four-beat walk
- two beat trot in diagonal pairs
- three beat canter

The quality of the paces can be improved as the horse learns to balance more on his hindlegs, but the paces much be correct and regular before these improvements can be made.

Soundness

Whatever discipline you want a horse for, it's crucial that the animal is sound and has "a leg at each corner."

In dressage, the regularity of the paces is essential, so any soundness issues are a deal-breaker.

As mentioned earlier in the book, not all racehorses retire unsound. In fact, racehorses receive more care and attention to their soundness than most ordinary riding horses!

Conformation

Dressage requires certain conformational characteristics in a horse. Although any horse can become more muscled and stronger with systematic training, there are a few things to look out for when viewing ex-racers.

Firstly, thoroughbreds are naturally built "on the forehand" with hind legs that are disproportionately longer than their front legs. This conformation is what helps to make them speed machines, however, dressage is about teaching a horse to work with engagement in a more uphill balance, so the less downhill he is naturally built, the easier it will be for you to bring him up off the forehand.

Secondly, horses that are overly long in the back often find it difficult to take weight behind, to bend around circles, and to ride together.

Thirdly, animals that have weak hocks may struggle to carry more weight on their hindquarters, and horses with a very upright shoulder will lack freedom of movement in the walk and medium paces.

Ideally, a horse that's intended for use as a dressage animal will have well-let down hocks, a sloping shoulder, be relatively short-coupled, and be built in proportion.

Although these are the ideals, it's important not to find too much fault in the horse's conformation, otherwise, you will never buy a horse at all!

Size

Big horses can look impressive and powerful, but they must be coordinated for you to be able to bring them on to the aids. They often need stronger, more precise aids and take longer to build their own strength to develop a good way of going and self-carriage.

A slight, petite rider is much better off on a smaller horse. The overall impression will be much nicer to look at.

The bottom line is that you don't need a huge, 17hh horse, and certainly not if you're only 5'2" tall!

So, choose a horse that is the right size for you so that you can balance him effectively and sit on him comfortably.

Temperament

If you are not use to racehorses, getting a gauge on a horse's temperament whilst he is still in training and race fit is not so easy. A horse that seems highly strung and difficult to handle could be the most laid-back plod after he has been "let down".

The horse's diet, training, and lifestyle all have a huge effect on the horse's temperament, and this should be taken into consideration when viewing a horse straight from the track. In these circumstances, it's advisable to take someone with you who is experienced with racehorses.

If you are viewing an ex-racer who has already been "let down" and has begun his re-training, then you will be able to get a better idea of what the horse's temperament is like. Ideally, you want a horse that is calm and sensible, willing to please, and enjoys learning.

Questions to ask

Many people are nervous or embarrassed about asking direct questions, such as, has the horse ever been lame, does it have any insurance exclusions, etc. **Don't be afraid to ask!**

It's a good idea to make a list of potential questions before you go to view the horse. This ensures that you find out everything you want to know on the day.

The more information you can gather about the horse's past life, the easier it will be for you to make an educated decision as to whether the horse will be suitable. It will also make the journey from racehorse to dressage horse much easier for the both of you.

Here are some questions that you can ask when viewing:

- When did the horse last race?
- What are the reasons for the horse's retirement/sale?
- How is he with the farrier, vet etc.?
- How was he to handle at the races?
- What is he currently being fed?
- Does the horse receive any supplements?
- When were his teeth last checked?
- What are the dates of his vaccinations?

- Does he have any vices?
- When was he last wormed?
- Has he had any injuries?
- What is his current daily routine and exercise schedule?
- Is he good to clip?
- Is he good to travel?
- How is he with other horses?
- How long does he spend in the field?
- Is he turned out in a paddock on his own or with other horses?
- Does he catch easily from the field?
- Has he been lunged/long-reined?
- Has he jumped?
- Has he been vetted before?
- Has he ever had colic?
- Does he have any health concerns?
- How is he to bath/groom?

If the person selling the horse is evasive or reluctant to answer any of your questions, walk away.

Riding the horse

Unless you are buying the horse straight from the racing yard, then you may be permitted to ride the horse. Many of the rehoming charities would have begun the re-training process before advertising the horse so the basic aids should have been established.

If you're not accustomed to riding strange horses, you may find trying your ex-racer a somewhat daunting experience, so, be sure to ask the current owner/trainer to ride the horse first. That will give you a good idea of what to expect. If they are reluctant to ride the horse, ask why!

When ridden, you want to see the horse in all paces and on both reins. Are there any signs of stiffness, tension, resistance, and irregularity of the paces? Is the horse obedient and willing to move forward? Does he stop when he's asked to?

When you ride the horse, make sure he stands quietly while you mount and moves off obediently and promptly when asked to do so. Remember that you're going to be riding this horse every day. If you feel at all nervous or worried about getting onboard or you can't wait to get off, this is not the horse for you!

You must be able to ride the horse and feel at home in the saddle when trying one out. The rideability of the horse is absolutely critical.

Vetting

No matter what the background or age of the horse, you should always have a pre-purchase veterinary examination carried out. That will help to flag any issues or health conditions of which you need to be aware before you part with your cash and get the horse home.

If geographically possible, it's a good idea to use your own vet or one who specializes in treating horses who has been recommended to you, ideally not by the person selling the horse!

A thorough vetting will involve checking the horse's eyesight, heart, and lungs. The vet will see the horse trotted up and may perform flexion tests on the animal's joints for signs of stiffness. If there are any areas of doubt, the vet may recommend that you have X-rays taken of the suspect joint.

Blood tests will also be taken to ensure that the horse has not been "doped" prior to the vetting.

If the vetting is clear and the horse passes with flying colors, you will have the peace of mind that you are not buying an unsound animal. Also, many insurance companies require that horses are vetted before they will agree to provide you with cover.

A small note about vetting

You should always prepare for ambivalence from the vet.

They may not 'fail' the horse, but they rarely get excited about a horse either, so you should be prepared to make your own judgment.

Many people have had years of good riding and companionship from a horse that has had a poor report from a vet.

Other things to note when viewing

- A horse that is currently still in training may look on the thin side and his belly may seem to be "tucked up". As the horse's diet and exercise regime changes, he will begin to fill out and look more "normal".
- Try to look for both the good and bad in every horse you view. It can be amazingly easy to fall in love with a horse and miss the red flags that could cause you trouble further down the line. On the flip side of the coin, if you are only looking for the imperfections you may overlook some great potential. So, make sure you are objective and look for both the good and bad equally.
- Don't be pressured in buying. If your gut is trying to tell you something, or other people are having to persuade you into it, then this is not the horse for you.
- Take your time. Although you're probably eager to get your new horse and crack on with your training, there is no rush. Don't buy a horse just for the sake of buying a horse.

SECTION THREE:
HOW TO RE-START AN EX-RACEHORSE

STEP 1: LETTING DOWN & HEALTH CHECKS

Thoroughbreds, by nature, are extremely sensitive. Their nerves are closer to the surface of the skin and since they have been purposely bred to race, they have a heightened flight response which can make them more reactive. And the fitter he is, the more responsive he can be. This is a good reason why, if your horse has come directly from a racing yard where he's been in full work, we advise letting the horse down before you begin re-training.

Letting down and settling in

The letting down period allows the horse to unwind from all the stresses of racing life.

How you handle this period will depend on the time of year, your yard facilities, and your own situation. However, the most important thing that you must remember is that the horse's life has been turned completely upside down and inside out by leaving the familiarity and routine of the racing world. An ex-racer will need plenty of time, and patience on your part, to settle into his new environment and routine.

Flat racers, in particular, have had very busy lives and have been ridden and worked from an early age. These horses never really had the chance to simply "be a horse."

After his letting down period is over, your OTTB will be much more relaxed and ready to start his re-training.

This is a mental transformation as much as it is a physical transformation.

Turnout

The best way of letting your horse down is to turn him out into a field. However, racehorses are accustomed to being looked after a great deal, therefore, if you immediately put him in a field to live, most are not going to understand this (or like it!).

You may also find that in the beginning he doesn't want to be out for long periods, so this is something that you can gradually increase over time. This is also advisable since some racehorses may not have had grass for a while and the last thing that you want to happen is for the horse to gorge and cause himself to colic.

So, before turnout, it's sensible to ask the horse's previous keeper whether the animal has been turned out before and, if so, for how long each day. You also need to know whether the horse has been turned out alone or in company.

Based on your findings, you can decide on the best turnout regimen for him. It's ideal if you can turn the horse out at grass all day, but if he's only used to going out for an hour each day, you'll need to gradually increase his turnout time.

It's also important to note that thoroughbreds are thin skinned and sensitive to the elements. They are used to wearing blankets and being inside out of the wind and rain. If you are turning out in less than ideal weather conditions, ensure that your horse is wearing a suitable rug to keep him comfortable.

A new routine

Horses in general thrive on a routine. This is especially true for your ex-racer who has been on strict routine for most of his life. For that reason, you can protect your ex-racer against stress by establishing a routine for him.

In the beginning, it's unlikely that your OTTB will be spending all day in the field as mentioned previously. So, for the time that he is in his stable introduce him to a new routine.

Make sure that is fed, mucked out, groomed, and turned out at the same time every day. If he knows what to expect at each time of the day, then he will be more likely to relax.

Equine company

Racehorses are very rarely on their own. They are stabled with other horses, they train with other horses, and they travel with other horses.

When you bring your new horse home for the first time, ensure that there are other horses around which he can take his cues from. Putting him into an empty stable barn whilst all the other horses are in the field for the day is not a good idea.

So, try to ensure that there is at least one other horse in eyesight at least for the first few days.

How long will it take to let him down?

This question is equivalent to 'how long is a piece of string?' Each horse is an individual and therefore each horse will take a different amount of time. Some horses will take a few months and others only a few weeks.

Your goal is to have your new equine friend in a relaxed and chilled-out mental state. The higher the horse's anxiety levels are when you receive the horse, the longer this is going to take to achieve.

You may find that some ex-racers struggle with this letting down period. They can become unhappy without a job and may show some signs of frustration. If this happens, it may be best to put the horse into some form of training. For example, twice a day you could carry out some basic in-hand work. Keep it light and easy so that you are resting the horse but still giving him something to think about. This will help to keep him calmer and happier.

Basic health checks

It's assumed that you have had the horse vetted prior to purchase. If he has come from a racehorse re-training center, the horse should come with a clean bill of health. That said, it does no harm to carry out your own health checks to ensure there are no problems which are going to hinder your re-training.

Here are some areas for you to pay attention to.

<u>Vaccinations</u>

Ensure that all your horse's vaccinations are up to date.

Contact your vet if you are in doubt as to what vaccinations are needed.

<u>Worming</u>

It's advisable to carry out a fecal worm egg count which will indicate whether the horse should be wormed.

If you are on a livery yard, you will also need to check the yard policy and make sure that you fit in with their regime.

<u>Teeth</u>

Most racehorses become stressed when they move to a new yard, and many have a tendency to drop weight. A few weeks out at grass is usually enough to encourage an improvement in condition, but it's sensible to ask an equine dentist to check the horse's teeth.

Sharp hooks or uneven tooth wear can be all it takes to prevent the horse from chewing his food properly and will almost certainly cause you a problem when it comes to bitting and riding your horse.

Hoof health

Racehorses can have a bad rep when it comes to their feet. Although it's true to say that some ex-racers have flat feet that can be weak, with good nutrition and a good farrier, the hoof health can be improved considerably, and the foot can be correctly balanced.

Now is the time to call your farrier who can help correct any potential issues and advise on how to improve hoof health.

Physio

As long as your new former racehorse has been vetted, you should be confident that he doesn't have any soundness issues. But if your horse has been in intense physical training, it's sensible to have an equine physio examine the horse to check that his back, neck, joints, and muscles are all in good order before you start any work.

Diet and nutrition

Before the horse arrives at your yard, try to find out as much as possible about his diet. You need to know what he was fed, how much he was fed, and at what times he was fed.

If your horse is coming straight from training, then he was most probably given three bucket feeds a day which were high in protein and high in energy.

Your job is to replace these feeds with fiber and forage, but it's important that you **make any changes to his diet gradually.** It can take two to three weeks for the microbes in your horse's digestive track to adjust to a new diet and return to normal function, and changing too quickly can cause all sorts of digestive upset. So, mix the two feeds for a week or so while gradually removing the grains and increasing the fiber.

If your ex-racer appears incredibly lean in comparison to the happy hackers and dressage horses in your yard when he arrives, don't make the mistake of overfeeding him. You should stick to the feeding routine with which he's comfortable and familiar. As the horse relaxes and begins to lose his high fitness levels, he will begin to fill-out and gain condition.

Don't panic too much if the horse seems to have a bad appetite for his hag/haylage in the beginning. As a racehorse he was used to eating huge amounts of grain which left him with little desire to eat his forage. As long as the horse has had his teeth checked and seems bright and well in himself, then he should come round in a few days.

Equine Gastric Ulcer Syndrome (EGUS)

Gastric ulcers are a surprisingly common complaint that can affect any breed, type, or age of horse. However, due to the feeding routine and stresses of racing, your OTTB is especially susceptible to them.

<u>What are gastric ulcers?</u>

In order to understand what causes gastric ulcers, it's necessary to understand a little about the physiology of the horse's stomach.

The horse has a small stomach relative to its size. In fact, the stomach is roughly the same size as a rugby ball.

The stomach is split into two areas, separated by a line called the *margo plicatus*.

- The upper area of the stomach (*squamous mucosa*) is lined with tissue that is similar in nature to that found inside of your mouth.
- The lower part (*glandular mucosa*) contains glands that secrete acid and has a protective mucosal layer.

Horses evolved to be 'trickle feeders', spending many hours wandering and foraging as they did so. Consequently, the equine stomach is designed to receive only small amounts of roughage at frequent intervals and to never be left completely empty.

Ulcers form in the horse's stomach as a direct result of exposure to excess gastric acid, which can occur if a horse is exercised on a completely empty stomach. The stomach acid is not restricted or soaked up by roughage in the horse's stomach and therefore splashes onto the tissue in the upper stomach that is not protected by a mucosal lining as the horse moves. The acid 'burns' the sensitive stomach wall, causing painful ulceration.

The severity of gastric ulcers can vary from tiny areas of inflammation to deep craters, filled with dead or dying tissue. Vets use a scoring system from 0 to 4 to grade the severity of the ulcers.

What are the causes of gastric ulcers?

There are a number of causes of EGUS including:

- feeding low forage/high concentrate diets
- long periods spent stabled with little or no forage intake

- intense exercise
- stress, e.g. from traveling
- lack of access to clean water

As you can see, it's highly likely that your ex-racer may suffer from gastric ulcers due to their lifestyle and feeding regime when racing. Therefore, it's very important that you recognise the signs.

What are the signs of gastric ulcers?

Here are some common signs of EGUS to watch out for:

- weight loss and poor appetite
- loss of condition and dull coat
- mild, recurrent colic
- stretching to urinate
- reduced or uncharacteristically poor ridden performance
- behavioral changes
- discomfort on having the girth tightened
- extra sensitivity during grooming

If your horse shows any of the above signs, speak to your vet about checking for and treating ulcers.

The treatment your horse will undergo will depend on the severity and type of his ulcers.

Preventing gastric ulcers

Correct, ongoing management of the horse is vital if ulcers are to be prevented.

You can start by ensuring that your horse receives good-quality hay or haylage ad-lib throughout the day and night or has access to good grazing, which can also help to reduce stress.

If the horse is stabled for much of the time, several small feeds during the day are better than one or two large ones and should be accompanied by ad-lib forage and plenty of fresh water.

STEP 2: HANDLING

Even though you are most likely not going to be riding your OTTB straight away, it's important to note that your re-training begins as soon as you get your new horse home.

So, even though this is "step 2" in the book, it's meant to be carried out alongside or overlapping step 1 since you will be handling the horse from the very first day he arrives.

As a racehorse, he's been handled quite a lot. Being led around is not a new thing for him. But you must start teaching him how you expect him to behave and set clear new boundaries of what is required of him. And this starts from you handling him from the ground.

Calm confidence

Racehorses are used to being handled by professionals who are confident, smooth, and deliberate with their movements. It's important that you approach and handle the horse in the same manner.

If you are nervous, uptight, or unsure of yourself, your horse will pick up on that and their flight instincts may tell them to resist and flee.

We are not advocating that you bully or push the horse around, but your movements should be steady, purposeful, and calm to give the horse confidence.

Positive early lessons

Remember that the horse has no idea he is no longer a racehorse and that his purpose and job have now changed. So, lots of patience is required to help your new partner acclimatize to his new life.

Keep the process as simple as possible and don't introduce too many changes at once as this could cause the horse to become anxious and scared.

Your ex-racer's early lessons should be kept short and sweet. Do a little at a time to build trust. If you have a problem or a setback, just go back a step or two and start over.

The thoroughbred is a highly intelligent and sensitive creature, so use this time to help build a solid foundation of trust and respect. Although you may be eager to get on a ride your new horse, the time you spend on the ground will help to set you up for success.

Building a harmonious partnership starts here.

Safety first

Safety comes first. When handling your horse always wear a hard hat, gloves, and suitable footwear.

Never wrap the lead rope around your hand and where possible, always use an enclosed arena that gives you enough space to get out of the way if necessary.

If, at any time, you are in doubt or nervous, then enlist the services of a professional to help you.

Leading

Some racehorses are accustomed to being led in a chain or even a Chifney.

A Chifney is also known as an anti-rearing bit. You'll often see racehorses being paraded at the racecourse in Chifney bits to give the handler more control. The bit's mouthpiece is a thin metal circle that loops over the horse's tongue and behind his chin. The Chifney is attached to a sliphead that can be easily slipped on and off.

Ideally, you shouldn't need to use a Chifney when leading your horse around the yard and to and from the field. However, if you do feel as though you need more control then you may find a Dually or some other variety of controller halter does the job just as well without being as severe in action. If you don't have access to one of those, then you can always use a simple bridle with snaffle bit.

Once your horse begins to relax and settle into his new routine, he will quickly learn to walk quietly at your shoulder when being led.

Tying and cross tying

Racehorses are generally not tied up outside their stables on racing yards, and it's highly unlikely that they have experienced cross ties.

That's partly for safety reasons, but it's also to prevent extra work for the busy lads and lasses who simply don't have time to sweep up any mess that's made outside on the yard.

So, your ex-racer must learn to be tied and to stand quietly.

<u>Tying</u>

The best place to introduce your horse to tying is directly outside of his stable in an area he is familiar with and feels comfortable. It also helps that there are other horses around him which are calm and relaxed.

Distract the horse with a haynet and begin by passing the rope through a piece of string attached to the tie ring. Once the horse accepts that, tie him with a quick-release knot in case he panics and pulls back.

Start by tying him up for only short periods and increase the time each day.

Don't walk off and leave him! Instead, use this time to give him a groom, straighten up his stable, top up his water etc.

Cross-ties

When first introducing your horse to cross-ties, do so when the yard is quiet.

Start by clipping on one cross tie and have an assistant hold the other cross tie and stand in front of the horse.

Talk to the horse and slowly groom him. Your goal is only to have him stand still for a few minutes then you can take him back to his stable. Don't keep him there too long as this new confined space may cause his anxiety levels to rise. Keep the sessions short and positive.

The next day repeat the exercise but for a bit longer.

Once your horse seems more comfortable, you can clip on the other cross tie, but still have your assistant stand in front of the horse. Once the horse has accepted that this is where he must stand, you will no longer need an assistant.

This process can take 7-10 days. You need to remain patient and only do a little bit every day. Rushing the horse or just 'tying him and leaving him' can be extremely dangerous. The horse could injure himself and have a negative experience that will be much harder to overcome.

Standing

Racehorses are not taught to stand still while being mounted. Usually, the jockey is legged up onto the horse as the animal is walking forward, and that applies on the yard as well as on the racecourse.

However, in the ordinary riding horse world, no-one wants a horse that walks off while you're trying to get on! So, teaching the ex-racer to stand still and understand voice commands, such as "whoa" or "stand" is important.

Use a voice command and gentle pressure to teach him to stop and stand still. Stand for just a few seconds before praising the horse and asking him to walk forward again. If the horse moves, correct him immediately. Gradually increase the length of standing time as the horse becomes more confident.

You can do this at various points around the arena and also positioned in front of the mounting block, so he knows what is expected of him when you're ready to climb aboard.

Grooming

Spending time one-on-one grooming your OTTB is a great way to build trust and relaxation.

Rather than rushing in with array of bushes and coat-shine spray, start by calmly running your hands all over horse to check for any sensitive areas.

Allow the horse to see and smell the bushes before first using it on his shoulder and then gradually working your way over the rest of his body.

Talking to your horse throughout this process is very beneficial. He will start to recognize your voice and you can teach him commands such as 'over' (for when you need him to move over) and 'stand' (for when you need him to stand still). When the time comes to ride him, he will be much more relaxed and happier when he recognizes the voice of the person who is on his back.

Trailering

Almost all racehorses are transported in lorries or small horseboxes rather than trailers. If you don't have the luxury of a lorry, your former racehorse must learn to go in a trailer.

This smaller and more confined space is new to him, so don't rush it and force him to get on. That will only cause more problems than it will solve.

Plenty of patience (and maybe a nanny horse) will help to get him on.

Depending on the trailer that you have, you can try dropping the front ramp so that the horse can see all the way through the trailer. This sometimes helps as the horse is no longer walking into a dark confined space.

It's also very important that the horse learns to stand quietly in the trailer or on the lorry. On race days, the horses are unloaded as soon as they arrive at the racecourse. They are taken straight from the lorry to the racecourse stables, where they chill-out for a few hours before racing.

So, your horse must learn to wait patiently in the trailer or lorry, as you won't have the luxury of a stable for him at most competition venues. Again, it's really just a matter of getting the horse used to waiting. Usually, a haynet is a sufficient distraction.

Start by calmly loading the horse and leaving him on the lorry or in the trailer for just a few minutes, gradually increasing the time as he begins to settle and stands quietly.

Also, be aware that your ex-racer may not have worn travel boots before, especially the big padded kind. If you want to use these types of boots for travel you'll need to give your horse time to get use to them.

STEP 3: FITTING TACK

Once your ex-racer has enjoyed his holiday, looks nicely covered, and is settled into his new home, you can start to think about the re-training process and starting his new career as a dressage horse.

In this section, we shall go through the various pieces of tack that you will need and how to fit them.

Fitting a new saddle

An ex-racer may not have experienced a general-purpose or dressage saddle before, especially if he has come directly from the track, and compared with a tiny racing saddle, a regular saddle will feel heavier and totally different.

Racehorses straight out of training will have a highly-toned, muscular body that is of a totally different shape to that of a riding horse. After his lifestyle change and as the re-schooling process progresses, the horse's body shape will change considerably. So, you'll need to employ a qualified, reputable saddle fitter to check the fit of your horse's saddle and make adjustments regularly.

Although you are advised to have your saddle fitted by a qualified saddle fitter, it's helpful if you have an understanding of the basics of how to fit a saddle. Here are nine fundamental points of saddle fitting are used by the Master Saddlers Association when training saddlers.

These nine points can be used as a basic checklist to identify a saddle's suitability for a particular horse and rider.

Before beginning your evaluation of the saddle's fit, make sure that the horse is standing square on a flat surface. Also, do not use a saddle pad or cloth. The saddle should fit the horse without any need for padding underneath it.

1. Saddle position

Start by placing the saddle gently on the horse's back, slightly forward on the withers. Place your hand on the horse's neck in front of the withers. Take the pommel with your right hand and pull the saddle sharply back and down. The saddle should "lock in" when it's in the correct position. Repeat the process to check that the saddle stops in the same place every time.

The saddle shouldn't sit too far forward, which would prevent the horse's shoulder from moving freely. When the horse moves, his shoulder blade (scapula) can move backward by up to three inches. The placement of the saddle must allow the saddle to clear the shoulder so that the horse can move freely. The saddle tree "points" should be far enough behind the horse's shoulder blade that they don't interfere with his movement.

If the saddle tree is the wrong size for the horse, it will move around, causing considerable discomfort when the horse moves forward with the rider on his back.

2. Saddle seat should be level

Once you have the saddle correctly placed on the horse's back, look at the deepest part of the seat. The deepest area of the saddle's seat should be centered between the pommel at the front and the cantle at the back.

The deepest part of the seat should be level. That allows you to sit correctly and effectively without placing too much pressure on the horse's back.

If the saddle's center point is too far forward, you'll slip forward toward the pommel. Your natural response to correct that is to brace against your leg, making your aids less effective.

If the deepest point of the saddle's seat is too far back, you'll slide backward toward the cantle, placing too much weight on the horse's back and causing him to hollow away from the discomfort. Also, when you ride in sitting trot, you'll find that you will tip forward onto your fork so that you don't feel as though you're being "left behind."

Sometimes, as long as the saddle's tree fits the horse correctly, it's possible to correct these problems by asking a qualified saddle-maker to adjust the panels.

3. Cantle-to-pommel relationship

The cantle of a dressage saddle is always higher than the pommel. That's because the design takes into account the amount of sitting trot that a dressage rider does.

So, the cantle always should conform to the anatomy of your seat.

However, provided the saddle tree fits the horse, if the saddle is too low behind you, your saddler may be able to boost the seat slightly by adding extra flocking to the back panel.

4. Clearance beneath the pommel

The saddle must give adequate clearance to the horse's withers so that it doesn't rub.

Place one of your hands perpendicular to the ground and slide it into place between the withers and the pommel. You should be able to fit two to three fingers into the space without difficulty.

So long as the saddle tree fits the horse correctly, a saddle fitter should be able to add extra flocking to balance the saddle properly to ensure that it clears the withers.

5. Point angles

The saddle tree's points determine the width of the saddle and dictate whether it fits correctly.

The saddle tree points are found in front of the billet straps, under the saddle flaps. You'll see what looks like a pocket. Inside this pocket, you'll find the points of the saddle.

Place the saddle on the horse and look at the angle of the saddle points relative to the angle of the horse's body. The points should be parallel to the horse's body or within ten degrees of parallel.

If the angle of the saddle points is too steep, the tree is too narrow. If the angle is larger, the saddle is too wide.

If the saddle tree doesn't fit the horse, it will cause discomfort. You can't alter a saddle tree, so if it doesn't fit the horse, you'll need to replace the saddle.

6. Panel pressure

Of course, a saddle might look like a good fit without the weight of a rider in it. But what happens when you apply pressure to the panels?

The saddle panels should be as big as possible to ensure even weight distribution.

Place the palm of your hand on the saddle and apply downward pressure. Use your other hand and run it from the top to the bottom of the saddle underneath the points to check that pressure is consistent throughout.

Now move your hand along the length of the panel, feeling for any points where the saddle doesn't touch the horse and areas of pressure. Be sure to check both sides of the saddle. Most ex-racehorses are not completely symmetrical, so ask your saddler to adjust the flocking in the panels if necessary.

Place one hand on the pommel and the other on the cantle and see if you can rock the saddle. If the saddle rocks back and forward like a seesaw, it's likely that the flocking is uneven and requires adjustment. Also, rocking can be caused by an ill-fitting saddle tree.

7. Gullet clearance

Stand behind your horse (if safe to do so) and look down the gullet of the saddle. The gullet should clear the whole length of the horse's spine without touching the back on either side.

Next, push down on the cantle and look again. Sometimes, if a horse is asymmetrical and you place weight on the saddle, it can shift over onto the spine, causing discomfort for the horse.

This problem can usually be corrected by adding some more flocking, adding a balance strap, or changing how the saddle is girthed.

8. Saddle length

The surface of the saddle that carries your weight should be between the horse's withers and the place where the last rib meets the spine. If your saddle rests too far behind this point, it will rest on the horse's lumbar region. That area is the weakest part of the horse's back, and the pressure of a rider's weight on this area can cause injury.

9. How the horse reacts

If a saddle fits correctly and is comfortable, the horse will move freely without hollowing, swishing his tail, or showing other signs of discomfort.

Girth the saddle but don't use a saddle pad or cloth, as that could prevent you from clearly seeing the fit of the saddle.

Once you are riding your ex-racehorses, here are some extra checks you need to make to ensure that the saddle fits.

- The pommel should clear the withers by two to three fingers
- A person on the ground should be able to see clear daylight running right down the length of the gullet when viewing the saddle from behind you
- The saddle should feel stable underneath you. You should feel balanced, not tipping forward or backward or struggling to sit up straight.
- When riding, the horse should be able to move freely, and he should be relaxed, showing no signs of resistance or tension.

How should the saddle fit the rider?

Now you know how the saddle should fit your horse, you'll need to be sure that it fits you properly too!

Dressage riders need to sit in a neutral, deep position in good balance. A good quality dressage saddle should have:

- A deep seat
- Long, straight flaps
- Thigh blocks
- Long girth straps

There are dozens of different styles of dressage saddle to choose from, and the one you're most comfortable with is largely a matter of personal preference. You might like a very deep seat with large knee blocks, or a shallower seat with smaller blocks might work better for you. Again, to accommodate individual body shape, you might prefer a saddle with a narrow twist or a wider one.

There are a few red flags that tell you immediately that you're in the wrong dressage saddle:

- You feel as though you're tipping forward
- You feel as though you're tipping backward
- You slide from pommel to cantle (seat is too big)
- Your seat overflows from the saddle's seat (seat is too small)
- You struggle to give leg aids as the saddle flaps are too long
- The saddle flaps catch on your boot tops (flaps are too short)
- You feel as though you are perching on the saddle because your leg is overhanging the knee block

Always make sure that the saddle fits BOTH you and your horse. It's no use having a saddle that fits your horse perfectly if you can't ride him in it!

Bitting

A common problem with ex-racers is that they can be reluctant to take a proper contact and work into the bridle. After all, they have not been taught this before. So, don't be concerned if you initially struggle to find a bit that suits your horse. Finding a bit that your horse is comfortable with can take a few attempts until you find the right one.

Using a bitless bridle is not always a practical or safe option in the horse's early days, as he has little understanding of the aids, especially the seat aid which is crucial when riding without a bit.

Choosing the shape/type of bit

Just in terms of snaffles, you need to choose:

- Straight, jointed, or double-jointed, and type of plate/lozenge in the latter.
- Straight or curved arms.
- Type/size of rings: loose, eggbutt, cheeked (half or full), hanging check, slotted etc.

Bear in mind that if you are riding under dressage rules, not all variations are 'dressage legal', so check the rules book of the organization that you intend you compete with before you try.

What bit should I choose?

It is not advised to put a harsh bit into an ex-racers mouth when re-training, even if he does seem on the strong side. A harsher bit can cause anxiety and tension and may leave the horse reluctant to connect with the contact. The best approach is to use a mild bit and to re-educate the horse on what is now expected of him and to re-school the mouth, rather than pressuring him into a forced submission. So, where possible and safe to do so, resist the urge to over-bit them.

In years past, bitting choices were limited. These days there is a bewildering array of shapes and sizes to choose from, and although hiring a bit from a 'bit bank' to trial how your horse gets on with your choice is a wonderful facility, you need to have some criteria in mind before you order.

Things to take into consideration when choosing a bit type are:

How does your horse accept the bit?

If his mouth is quiet, you may choose a loose ring snaffle for a more refined contact; if he is fussy, you might want an eggbutt or a full cheek snaffle for more stability.

The interior size of your horse's mouth

Does he have a low palette, a large tongue, or generally small mouth? If so, you will need a thinner mouthpiece.

Traditionally, we used to consider a fatter mouthpiece to be kinder, but these days studies have shown that the interior volume of a horse's mouth is smaller than we originally believed, making thinner bits actually more comfortable for many horses, rather than sharper.

Does your horse have fleshy lips?

An eggbutt or cheek snaffle is probably the better option to prevent potential pinching which you may get with a loose ring.

How long is your horse's mouth?

Some horse's lips come further up their cheeks than others – a shallow mouth might make a slightly curved mouthpiece a better choice, so the bit doesn't hang too low inside the mouth and risks him getting his tongue over it.

If he is a gelding (or stallion), where are his tushes situated?

Again, a fatter mouthpiece might cause the bit to knock against the tushes and cause discomfort. A thinner mouthpiece with a curved shape might be your best choice.

What width of bit do you need?

It should be as wide as his mouth plus a little, to allow it not to pinch the corners of the lips, but not so wide that (assuming it is a jointed bit) when rein contact is applied, the joint(s) do not bring the center of the bit too low inside the mouth, where he might be able to put his tongue over it.

Fitting the bit

Assuming you have chosen a shape and type that is suitable for your horse's individual mouth, when you attach it to your bridle it should hang at a height in his mouth so that:

- It just wrinkles the corners of his lips, and you do not struggle with sliding the headpiece over his ears when you put the bride on.
- Is not so low that it either knocks against his tushes (male horse), or permits him to pull his tongue up and put it over the bit, or, if single jointed, that the joint knocks into the rear of his incisors (front teeth) when a rein contact is applied.
- If the width is correct, it should lie just loosely enough within his mouth that you can slide it to one side and see only about one or two centimeters of the mouthpiece showing on the opposite side.

Bitting experts

There are so many possibilities these days, it may be worth your while asking the advice of one of the bitting companies, either at a clinic or by filling in an online questionnaire.

Remember that much scientific research done in recent years has disproven traditional beliefs about bit fitting, and with so many variations of shape and mouthpiece thickness available on today's market, asking for expert advice is often a good choice.

Once you've made your choice, fitting the bit to your bridle is a matter of finding a comfortable height that is neither too high (tight when you try to slide the bridle over the ears), or too low where it might cause tongue or teeth issues.

Nosebands

Clearly, the bit you choose has an influence on the quality of the contact that you have with your horse. But did you know that the style of noseband and how it's fitted can impact on the contact too?

An incorrectly fitted noseband of any style has an effect on much more than the horse's mouth. It can interfere with the horse's ability to carry himself.

In ideal circumstances, the rider's aids channel the energy generated by the horse's hind legs through his back and neck toward the rider's hands and the bit. A good rider then uses well-timed half-halts to create engagement, impulsion, and collection. When this process is working correctly, the horse develops self-carriage and becomes lighter in his forehand.

The noseband is not there to clamp the horse's mouth shut! That is cruel to the horse and usually leads to resistance and tension. A tight noseband can cause the horse to clench his jaws and grab the bit, making him heavy in the rider's hands, and encouraging the horse to lean on his shoulders and take more weight onto his forehand. In this scenario, it is possible for a strong rider to forcibly lift the horse's head and neck. However, that simply forces the horse into a false self-carriage ("absolute elevation") that only gives the impression of being uphill, rather than genuine self-carriage ("relative elevation").

A noseband that's too loose can interfere with a horse's ability to work in self-carriage as much as one that's too tight. If the noseband is too loose, the rider will have problems creating and maintaining a consistent connection. That can cause the horse's neck to wobble both longitudinally and laterally.

The horse will avoid the rider's half-halts by stiffening and lifting his head and becoming hollow behind his withers. An on-off connection usually causes tension in the horse, making it impossible for throughness to develop. Many riders become too busy or strong with their hands in an attempt to obtain submission from the horse, and a vicious circle is born.

What noseband to choose?

Racehorses are generally ridden in a plain cavesson noseband. However, you'll also see racers wearing what's called an Australian noseband, or cheeker. An Australian noseband is made from rubber and buckles to the headpiece of the bridle. These nosebands are designed to prevent the horse from getting his tongue over the bit and to control hard-pullers.

Ideally, you should ride your horse in a plain, padded cavesson noseband. Do not try to take shortcuts by forcing the horse's mouth shut with a flash or drop noseband, as that will most likely cause the horse to become stressed and may make the problems worse. If you horse does open his mouth whilst being ridden, we will show you how to correct this issue later on page 166.

How to fit a cavesson noseband

A cavesson noseband should be fitted so that it sits about 2cm below the bony facial crest so that it doesn't rub on the bone.

The noseband should be adjusted so that you can comfortably slide your thumb beneath it when the noseband is fastened.

Tuck any extra strap into the keepers at the back of the noseband so that it doesn't flap around and irritate the horse.

Martingales

For safety reasons, it's a good idea to fit a running martingale when you first start ridden work with your ex-racer. In a situation where your brakes fail, the last thing you want is for your horse to get his head above the point where you can control him and take off with you!

When the horse is working nicely, the running martingale with have no effect.

Breastgirth

It's likely that your ex-racer will not have much topline muscle and that can allow the saddle to slip backward.

If you think that this might be a problem, fitting a breastgirth will help to prevent that problem until your horse builds sufficient muscle.

Your saddle fitter will be able to advise you on this.

Boots

Whether you're working with your ex-racer from the ground or in the saddle, you should fit him with brushing and overreach boots. That will protect the horse from accidental injury and a frustrating lay-off if he loses his balance and treads on himself.

When first fitting boots, be aware that he may have not worn boots before so give him time to walk around in them and get used to them first.

A note about draw reins and other training aids

We do not advise the use of draw reins or similar training aids such as bungees, de gogues, chambons, etc. when re-training your ex-racehorse for dressage.

Your goal in dressage is to train the horse to seek the bit and to connect to the bit. Training aids such as the aforementioned are designed to put pressure on the bit and on the horse's poll to help "teach" the horse how to "carry his head correctly".

However, using these training aids often results in a horse that drops his poll and curls up behind the vertical. The horse works with a tight, hollow back with his hocks trailing, and will most likely be on the forehand too.

Dressage is about developing the horse's natural athletic ability through correct, systematic training, and working patiently through the Scales of Training. The false outline that these training aids can create goes against all these aspirations and training principles, and that's why we don't condone their use.

STEP 4: LUNGEING AND LONG-REINING

Before climbing aboard, it's advised that you start your re-training from the ground and begin by lungeing and/or long-reining your OTTB.

If you have never lunged or long-reined before, your new ex-racer is not the horse for you to learn with. Instead, learn how to lunge with a more experienced horse first or get an experienced professional to do it for you.

Remember to keep the lessons short and ensure that your horse stays relaxed and happy throughout. Both long-reining and lungeing can be very strenuous for the horse, both mentally and physically, and having him whizz around too fast on a small circle can put a lot of pressure on the horse's joints and can cause injury and/or soreness.

Safety first

When long-reining or lungeing, always wear gloves, a hard hat, and suitable footwear.

Equipment needed

Bridle

Take the reins off or twist them up in the throatlatch so that the horse can't tread on them.

For long-reining you can leave the bridle as is, but for lungeing you may want to remove the noseband and replace it with a lunge cavesson.

Saddle or roller

If lungeing and using a saddle, run the stirrup irons up the leathers and wrap the loose ends of the leathers around the irons so that they don't slip down while the horse is moving. For long-reining, leave the stirrups down and secure them with a strap underneath the horse's girth area.

Alternatively, you can use a roller.

Boots

A pair of brushing boots and over-reach boots are advisable to prevent injury if the horse becomes unbalanced and accidentally treads on himself.

Lunge line(s)

For lungeing you will need one lunge line. For long-reining, you will need two lunge lines.

Your line(s) should be at least 33 feet long (10 meters). You can choose from webbing, rope, or nylon lunge lines.

Lunge whip

When lungeing, a long whip is necessary to guide the horse out onto circles and to keep him moving forward. When long-reining, it's likely that you will have your hands full enough so carrying a lunge whip is optional.

NOTE: The lunge whip should never be used to punish the horse.

Where should you lunge/long-rein?

When deciding where to work your horse, safety for both parties must be your main priority. Avoid surfaces that are slippery, boggy, uneven, rutted, very dry and hard, or on a steep incline/decline. Ideally, the area should be enclosed and flat with a suitable, cushioned surface. It's best not to work in an open field in case something startles your horse into flight mode.

For lungeing, a round pen is ideal, but if you don't have one an enclosed arena is also suitable.

For long-reining, always begin in an arena or enclosed space until you have an idea of what your horse is likely to do. Once you are both more confident, you can work in different areas, such as around the field or yard.

Give your ex-racer confidence

Most ex-racers will have been lunged and/or long-reined as part of the breaking process, so this is another element of the horse's training in which he may feel confident. However, if you are unsure, always air on the side of caution just in case this is your horse's first time.

To help give him confidence, organize for someone to help you, firstly to hold the horse while you get organized, and then to walk alongside him.

Racehorses are accustomed to working in company with other horses, so having a handler or another horse to follow or walk alongside will help to give your ex-racer confidence and make him feel secure. As your new horse grows in confidence, be sure to ask him to take the lead and work as leading file too.

Benefits of lungeing and long-reining

Lungeing and long-reining your OTTB has many benefits, including:

- Improving the horse's balance
- Improving the horse's rhythm

- Encourage relaxation
- Improving transitions between and within the paces
- Creating a firm foundation before riding
- Teaching voice commands
- Improving the horse's coordination
- Creating a rapport between horse and handler
- Enabling you to watch how the horse moves and carries himself, so that you can identify areas for improvement under saddle later on.
- Teaches the horse to work forward through his back and into an elastic contact and build muscle over the horse's topline
- Can increase rider confidence
- Introduces the horse to the feel of a bit and rein contact
- Teaches the horse aids for starting, stopping, and changing direction
- Can be used to desensitize spooky horses to unfamiliar sights and sounds

Things to note before you start

- Lungeing and long-reining can be hard work for the horse and going too fast and/or being out of balance will take its toll on your horse's limbs.
- Aim to create nice big circles of 20-meters. Having a horse work on a small 10-meter circle is very strenuous for the horse.
- Keep the sessions short and simple. Walking and halting for the first few sessions is a good idea as this will help keep the horse relaxed and help him to understand your voice commands and tone.
- When racing, the horses have been trained to go from zero to racing speed, so it's not uncommon for them to gain speed on a circle. Your horse will also struggle for balance, and the only way he knows how to balance himself is through momentum, so he may speed up.
- When using voice commands try to use the tone of your voice to tell the horse what you mean. For example, when asking for an upward

transition, raise the pitch of your voice at the end of your command. For a downward transition, make the command long, drawn-out, and in a lower pitched tone.

- If your horse becomes distracted or anxious with a task, you should back off the pressure, ask for only small steps of progress, give lots of verbal praise, and ask the horse to do something he is confident and familiar with. You can then go back to the new lesson later in smaller increments.

Lungeing

When lungeing, you stay in the center of the arena whilst the horse works on a large circle around you.

<u>How to lunge</u>

1. Before you start, make sure that the horse is not afraid of the lunge whip. Have the horse stand while you calmly touch the lunge whip on his shoulder and then all over his body. The horse should stay relaxed and comfortable.

2. Now, encourage the horse out onto a circle. To do this, lead the horse on a small circle with your lunge line in your outside hand, and the lunge whip tucked under your outside arm. Encourage the horse to walk forward, and then slowly move the lunge whip into your inside hand by grabbing hold of it behind your back.

    Bring the whip around and toward the horse's hindquarters, still encouraging him to move forward. Turn to face the horse, standing slightly behind his shoulder.

3. When lungeing, don't step back away from the horse; he will probably follow you in an ever-decreasing circle! Instead, step towards the

horse, using your body to ask him to move away from you and back out onto the circle.

4. Think of a triangle that's made by the horse, the lunge line, and the lunge whip. The horse forms the base of the triangle. The lunge line is one long side. And the whip is the other long side. Keep your body level with the horse's quarters so that you are in a driving position where there is less chance that the horse will stop and turn in towards you.

5. Keep your lunge whip up, and point it towards the horse's inside hock, without allowing the lunge line to trail on the floor. Once you've started and the triangle is formed, keep still, and move around the circle with the horse.

6. Your horse may fall in at the shoulder and drift toward you, creating a smaller circle. Point the whip at the horse's shoulder and step towards him, pushing him out onto the circle while keeping the lunge line tight.

7. If your horse begins to hurry, point your whip in front of him. That should slow him down. Use a slow, calm tone to encourage the horse to slow down and relax.

8. If your horse is lazy and won't go forwards, you need to shorten the lunge line and walk towards him. The circle should remain the same size, but you'll be closer to the horse. Point the whip at the horse's bottom and make encouraging noises to wake him up!

How to use side reins

Side reins are used to encourage the horse to work forward into a contact. They are not there to hold his head down or force him to work with an artificially low head carriage! When used correctly, the side reins will be the first step in re-schooling your OTTB's mouth. It will help him to build trust in the contact and encourage him to start reaching for the bit.

Side reins should have an elasticated insert to prevent the horse from fixing on the contact. They should have a buckle at one end so that you can adjust the length of the rein. The other end should have a spring clip, enabling you to fix the rein to the horse's bit.

Before you fit your side reins, allow the horse to warm up on both reins. Once the horse is happy and relaxed you can fit a pair of side reins. The most important point to remember when using side reins is that their job is to provide a light contact for the horse to work into.

Lungeing progression

Introducing poles

If you would like to use poles when lungeing, start with a single pole and allow the horse to walk over it in both directions first.

Poles will encourage the horse to look and think about where he is putting his feet. They will help to engage his hind legs, stretch his topline, and improve his suppleness. He will learn to balance himself, as well as becoming more flexible and coordinated.

Dropping the stirrups

At this stage, you won't have ridden your ex-racer. If you lunge your horse in his saddle, that can be a very useful way of getting the horse accustomed to the sound and feel of the saddle moving on his back.

Also, you can drop the stirrups down so that they rest on the saddle flaps.

As the horse trots, he will feel the stirrups moving, which is a great way of preparing your ex-racer for the feel of a longer leg than he is accustomed to.

Long-reining

When long-reining, you are positioned behind the horse, holding a lunge line in each hand just like a set of reins. In theory, long-reining can be likened to riding from the ground and you do need a fair degree of feel, a correct contact, and the correct body position for the exercise to work as it should.

Long-reining is generally used as the next step up from lungeing the horse before ridden work begins. So, by the time someone gets on the horse's back, he has a good understanding of the basic aids, including the voice. Long-reining can also be used to iron out problems that may present themselves before the horse is ridden.

You can begin long-reining your horse when he's confident and obedient on the lunge, as he will be comfortable with wearing a bridle, roller, or saddle, and he will be familiar with your voice commands.

When you first begin long-reining your horse, always recruit someone experienced and confident to help you from the ground.

<u>Getting started</u>

First, you'll need to get your horse organized and accepting two lunge reins. Have your assistant hold your horse with the lunge line attached to the nearside bit ring. Attach the other lunge line to the offside bit ring and thread it through the offside stirrup or through a loop in the roller.

Pass the second lunge line onto the horse's side so that it runs behind the saddle or roller and alongside the offside hind leg. Some horses become upset when they feel the lunge rein on their side. If your horse is worried by that, lift the lunge rein away from the horse right away, while your helper reassures the horse. Repeat the process until the horse accepts the lunge line and relaxes.

Now, position yourself on the horse's left side, and rest the second lunge line over the horse's croup. Ask the horse to walk forward, allowing the rein to drop over the croup and behind the horse.

Keep the initial sessions to around ten minutes, gradually increasing them to half an hour or so.

Walking-on and halt

To ask the horse to walk forward, gently tap his sides with the reins, and use your voice to say, "walk on."

To halt, ask the horse to "stand" or "whoa." At the same time, incline your upper body back slightly and apply a small amount of pressure with the reins until the horse stops. Immediately release the pressure and wait a few seconds before asking the horse to walk on again.

Straightness

If your horse tends to wander off a straight line, try setting two parallel ground poles as "tramlines" and drive your horse between them.

Practice halting between the poles, too, as a great way of teaching the horse to halt straight.

Trot and canter

On a circle, you can work the horse in trot and canter. Effectively, you're simply lungeing with two lunge lines. Keeping the outside line around the horse's body prevents him from falling out and to help you to engage his hindquarters by keeping him straighter on the circle.

Take up a position where you are standing parallel to your horse, facing his girth. Lunge the horse on a circle around you, keeping the outside line loose to avoid frightening or upsetting your horse. Walk around on a small circle and keep the contact the same as you did when you were walking behind the horse.

Here is where you can use a lunge whip and encourage the horse to trot and canter by using your usual lungeing aids.

<u>Finishing the session</u>

When you've finished your long-reining session, gently and slowly bring the right rein over the horse's back and approach his left side. Stand by the horse's head. You can then unclip the lunge lines from the bit and draw them through the stirrups or roller.

Long-reining problems

There are a few problems that can crop up when long-reining. Here's how to deal with them:

<u>Not moving forward</u>

If your horse ambles forward with a lack of activity, flick the lunge lines against his sides to mimic your leg aids. Encourage the horse to move forward by using your voice and make lots of transitions to keep his attention.

If the horse is still dawdling, try using a long whip, and tap it against your boot to back up your other aids.

Too much energy!

If you have the opposite problem and your horse is running away with you, regulate your own pace, and walk slowly. Make plenty of transitions back to halt, and include plenty of changes of rein, softening the rein through each turn as you would if you were in the saddle.

Don't pull back constantly on the reins or you'll end up in a tug-of-war that you can't win! Instead, squeeze the inside rein to soften the horse's jaw, and use your weight to "ride" a half-halt with the outside rein.

Be prepared to bring the horse onto a small circle if he tries to trot or take off with you! If necessary, use the corners of the arena as a brake.

Long-rein progression

When your horse is long-reining confidently you can use this tool to improve your horse's proprioception. Proprioception is the term used to describe the sense of recognizing where all the parts of the body are positioned at any given time. It's the sense that allows you to walk in the dark without falling over.

You can improve your horse's physical coordination, build trust, and encourage cooperation by incorporating patterns of movement into your long-reining sessions.

Walking the horse over poles and around obstacles helps to improve his balance and coordination while encouraging him to learn in a relaxed state. It's also a wonderful tool that you can use for introducing your ex-racer to potentially scary objects in a controlled environment before you venture out onto the roads and trails under saddle.

In the arena, try setting out different hazards, such as tarps, poles, flags standing in cones or buckets of sand, banners, balloons attached to the fence, etc. Long-rein the horse around your obstacle course until he's confident and settled.

Make sure you introduce one thing at a time. Turning your arena into a fairground attraction overnight can result in sensory overload and can spoil your otherwise calm and relaxed work.

How long do you need to lunge/long-rein for before riding?

There is no real timetable for this, however, as a general rule, your ex-racehorse will be ready to move onto the early ridden work when he is lungeing and/or long-reining calmly and confidently in all three paces and on both reins.

Each horse is an individual and you will have to listen to your horse and make your own judgement. Temperament, previous training styles, conformation, and physical strengths will dictate the journey you take.

STEP 5: EARLY RIDDEN WORK

Before starting ridden work, it's advised that:

- your horse is fully let down and has had a health check (step 1),
- he is calm and relaxed when handling (step 2),
- he has suitable tack that fits him correctly (step 3),
- and he lunges/long-reins comfortably on both reins and in all three paces (step 4).

Once you have all those four boxes ticked, you can then start ridden work.

Notes before you begin

Remember that your ex-racer has been trained to do a very particular job. When you begin riding him, you won't be painting on a blank canvas, but rather a canvas whose existing picture you'll first need to erase! The horse will not have forgotten his previous racing training. He may have lost fitness and now be calmer thanks to his lifestyle change, but that doesn't change what the horse knows.

You'll need to be consistent, patient, and kind, to show your ex-racer what you want from the new aids he is learning. If your horse rushes and tries to run on, that's most likely because he doesn't understand just yet.

As with all of your training, make sure that you reward every tiny step forward that the horse makes. Thoroughbreds are very sensitive by nature and praising your horse and telling him how clever he is, no matter how small the progress he makes, will help to keep your ex-racer happy and relaxed, rather than making him nervous and anxious. Your goal is for him to feel successful at the end of every training session.

Keep calm

Racehorses are ridden by confident jockeys and have no experience with nervous or tense riders. Therefore, it's important that you stay relaxed and calm to ensure that the horse also stays relaxed and calm.

Your aids

When riding these athletes for the first time, many riders can be too heavy with the aids and ask the horse too many questions in quick succession, which can turn into "nagging". This can cause the horse to become confused, anxious, and/or annoyed. Instead, keep your aids simple, clear, and light.

Your OTTB wants to do nothing more than to please you. So, if you are a "busy" rider and try to ask the horse to do seven things at once, the horse will most likely try to interpret and execute on all seven things getting themselves in a flustered mess.

Instead, keep the horse relaxed and introduce new aids one at a time in a simple and methodical process. You should make the process easy for the horse and set him up for success.

Balance and bodyweight

Your ex-racer has been taught to balance. Although it was a different type of balance, the horse will still pick up on cues from your bodyweight as this was the main means of communication between him and his jockey. You can use this to your advantage during your training.

Using new muscles

Give your horse plenty of time to adapt to this new way of carrying his rider. Think about what it's like for you when you do a new exercise. The same is true for your horse. He will be engaging muscles that he's never really used before and this can cause the muscles to fatigue quickly and become sore. This is a good reason to keep your first sessions short. If he answers all your questions correctly, it's wise to stop for the day rather than drilling him and making him sour and sore from the whole experience.

Avoid small circles

Your horse has not yet developed the muscles needed to balance and work in such a confined space. Therefore, keep your circles large and avoid any sudden changes of direction.

It can be extremely easy to overdo it on your first few rides, especially if you are eager to just crack on!

Keep other horses in sight

Racehorse are trained in the company of other horses. Therefore, it's advised to have other horses around for your first few rides to help put him at ease.

Do not try to fix problems

For the first couple of weeks, when the horse first comes back into work after his settling-in period, there will most likely be some problems with his way of going. For example, your ex-racer may be stiffer to one side than to the other, but don't be tempted to concentrate on the problem rein. Be sure to work both sides equally.

Now is not the time to try and correct issues. The goal of your first few rides together should be enjoyable and relaxing for both parties. The harder questions can come later.

Forget about "on the bit"

In these very early stages, there is no need to worry yourself about where your horse's head is or to try riding him "on the bit." He won't have developed the strength needed to correctly demonstrate self-carriage, therefore, any attempts that you do make will only result in a false and incorrect outline.

Look out for positive and negative signs

At every stage of training you need to listen to your horse.

If training is going well, you will have a calm and co-operative horse at each stage. If you have to 'force' the horse or if the horse starts to show heightened anxiety levels, then you know you are asking for too much too soon. In these cases, you need to take a step back, think about what happened, and try a different approach.

When things go wrong

If something doesn't go to plan, do not keep asking the horse the same question in the same way over and over again. If he didn't give you the correct answer the first three times you asked, what makes you think he will get it right the fourth time?

Instead, stop and ask yourself the following three questions:

1. Are you being clear?
2. Does the horse understand what you're asking?
3. Are there any physical reasons why he can't do it?

Most issues are due to a breakdown in communication.

Time and patience by the bucket load!

There are no short cuts when it comes to providing your horse with a solid foundation from which you can both build upon. Any short cuts that you do take you will pay for later down the line.

You are redeveloping your horse both mentally and physically. When done right, this process takes time.

Step 1 - Mounting

Racehorses are usually walking when the jockey is legged up. So, your horse won't understand that he must stand still while you mount.

If you completed the "Handling" chapter in this book, you will have spent some time teaching the horse to stand still from the ground next to the mounting block. Now all you need to do is repeat the lesson for real so that you can get on board safely.

To begin teaching your ex-racer to stand while you mount-up, it's a good idea to ask an assistant to help and hold the horse for you.

Mount-up smoothly but efficiently and sink down gently into the saddle rather than landing with a bump. Keep the reins loose and resist the urge to gather them up tightly.

If the horse walks forward, calmly correct him and ask him to stand again whilst using the same verbal commands you taught him on the ground.

Once you are on and he is standing still, pat the horse before asking him to calmly walk forward.

The whole process should be treated as "no big deal".

In situations where the horse's level of tension rises the longer he is asked to stand still, it may be prudent to get on and allow the horse to walk forward shortly after. The longer you ask the horse to stand still the more stress you could cause. You can improve on this by asking the horse to stand still for a little bit longer each time you mount.

Step 2 - Walking on and accepting the leg

When asking the horse to move forward away from your leg, use the voice commands that you use when long-reining and lungeing.

Apply the correct leg aids but remember that your leg and bodyweight will feel very strange to an ex-racer, and he may not understand what you are asking of him at first.

Be very gentle with your legs and don't try to take up a strong contact with your hands. It doesn't matter if the horse is straight or even if he jogs for a few steps. Reward him for moving forward. Gradually, you can place less emphasis on your voice and more on your leg.

If your horse shoots abruptly forward, don't take your leg off. Instead, keep them passively on the horse's sides. Let the horse understand that your leg is now a constant part of his new career, and it's something he must get used to from the get-go.

Step 3 – Halting

Now you're walking forward, the next step to establish the halt using the correct aids. Don't worry about anything else at this stage. All you need to achieve is that horse stands still when asked, even if that is just for a few seconds initially.

Here's another area where the voice commands come in that you taught your horse when working him from the ground. Use your voice, in conjunction with your seat, legs, and reins, to ask the horse to halt. As soon as the horse yields to your aids, release the pressure, and reward him.

Initially, when asked to halt, many ex-racers might step sideways, jog, walk backward, shake their heads, or even paw at the ground. Ignore these behaviors and quietly repeat your request for the horse to stop. When he finally does, reward him and allow him to walk forward.

Don't try to keep the halt for too long at first, or you could end up in a confrontational situation that could undo all your good work.

Step 4 – Repeat steps 2 and 3

Although this may sound boring, your first riding sessions will predominantly be in walk repeating steps 2 and 3. So, asking the horse to walk forward, asking the horse to halt, and repeating. Through this exercise you are instilling the basic "go" and "whoa" aids.

Your goal is to have the walk marching purposefully forward, encouraging the horse to use his whole body. Keep your rein contact elastic but not loose. Thoroughbreds like to have a contact, but keep your elbows, wrists, and hands soft to encourage the horse to stretch through his back, rather than attempting to hold him in an outline. That will help the horse to relax.

To keep the horse's attention, use the whole arena and ride various shapes and movements including large circles, serpentines, and changes of rein.

Step 5 - Trotting

Once you know that you can stop and start whenever you want to and the horse accepts your aids happily, you can start to introduce some trot work.

You'll probably find that the horse drifts over toward the outside of the school. Use your leg and voice to ride him forward and to help keep him straight.

In these early days, you should only be doing rising trot to allow the horse to use his back. Keep your rise steady and consistent and in a suitable tempo so that the horse can settle into a good rhythm.

Racehorses are accustomed to trotting for a few steps and then breaking into canter. If your horse decides that he would prefer to canter than trot, don't get into an argument. Keep calm and ride a large circle to prevent the horse from picking up speed and bring him back to trot.

Step 6 - Cantering

It's important to note that cantering and galloping are not the same. A racehorse has been taught how to gallop; he has not been taught how to canter.

Galloping involves the horse using momentum and balancing on his forehand using his head and neck. Whereas cantering involves engaging the horse's hindquarters, adopting a degree of self-carriage and a whole new center of balance.

Therefore, don't expect your horse to be able to canter in balance, in the small confines of a dressage arena, and with your additional weight as a rider, first time out. Your OTTB must undergo a fair amount of muscle development and re-balancing before he is able to achieve this.

Ideally, you would have started to teach your horse how to canter and balance on the lunge before adding your weight into the mix. When your horse is comfortable with this, you can introduce canter to his ridden work.

When introducing the canter, don't make a big deal out of the trot-canter transition. Instead, ride it as smoothly as you can, almost so that the horse doesn't realize it. Approach the exercise as you would when training a young horse that's cantering for the very first time. Don't worry if the horse runs into the canter or strikes off on the wrong lead. You can work on that later.

When in the canter, allow the horse freedom to work out what he's doing with his legs, and settle him into a steady rhythm and tempo using your seat and weight aids.

Do not take a tight hold on the reins. Racehorses are taught to go faster when the jockey puts more weight into the bridle. If you pull back on the reins, your horse will most likely just set against you. Ex-racers will very often come back to you quicker if you lighten the contact and allow the reins to gradually slip through your fingers.

The rider's balance

Jockeys and exercise riders are ultra-lightweight, especially those who ride flat racers. If you study the jockey's position, you'll notice just how different that is from that of a dressage rider.

The weight distribution and balance of someone riding "normally" will feel totally alien to the ex-racer. So, in the early days, it can be helpful to ride in "jockey dressage" mode.

<u>Finding the balance of a jockey</u>

Jockeys and exercise riders balance over their feet, allowing their ankles, knees, and hips to absorb the horse's movement, while their upper bodies remain motionless. To slow down, they lock their joints, releasing them to allow the horse to go forward. The rider's hands are placed on the horse's neck in front of the withers.

Try the following exercise, using a jump or forward-cut GP saddle if you have one that fits your ex-racer.

1. Stand up in your stirrups in halt. Your stirrups must be short enough so that your seat clears the pommel when you're standing up.

2. Stand on your toes, letting your heel drop down without losing your balance and dropping back into the saddle. Don't balance on your hands!

3. Now walk on. Place your hands on the horse's neck, slightly in front of the withers, resting your fists on the horse's neck close to the crest. You can cross your thumbs over the horse's mane, creating a bridge that prevents the horse from pulling you off over his neck. Try to stay balanced over your feet without relying on the horse's neck for support.

4. Go forward into trot, maintaining that position. Feel your ankles, knees, and hips acting as shock absorbers.

5. Ride a transition to walk by locking your knees and hips.

6. Once you've got the hang of that, try a few transitions and a little bit of canter.

Don't be surprised if your ex-racer settles into a nice rhythm and finds his balance. Using this technique helps the former racehorse to redefine his understanding of balance within his comfort zone.

"Jockey dressage"

Now let's try a bit of what we can call "jockey dressage."

Again, if possible, use a jump saddle or a forward-cut GP, rather than a dressage saddle. Pull the stirrups up as you did in the previous exercise.

1. Start by finding your balance over the feet, ensuring that your hands stay independent of your body and keep them connected to the bit, using the same feel as you do when schooling a dressage horse.

   If necessary, use the horse's neck for balance but only briefly. Before moving to the next step, you must be able to keep your balance without falling back onto your seat or pulling on the reins.

2. Ride the horse in walk, trot, and canter, aiming for the same frame that you would for Prelim or Training level dressage.

   Ride the horse between leg and hand just as you would in a dressage saddle. Using your leg and maintaining the connection in the contact is extremely difficult when you're effectively riding in a two-point eventer's seat, but you must persevere.

3. Ride some upward transitions from walk to trot and from trot to canter. You still need to use your lower leg, but you will find that you lean forward a little more in each transition to keep yourself from falling backward.

   If you can keep your balance, that leaning forward can be used as an aid to ask the horse to go more forward.

4. Ride a few downward transitions. Don't lean backward! Hold yourself a little taller, lock your hips and knees, and keep your balance.

Obviously, you want to transfer yourself back into your comfy dressage saddle at the earliest opportunity. However, when you first begin schooling your ex-racer, it can be helpful to keep him in his comfort zone as he learns the new aids and requirements of his new job.

How to create bend

Although racehorses may run on a slight curve, it's not the same as 'equal bend though the body'. Instead, they run straight because straight is faster, therefore, they are not very supple from side to side (laterally).

Bending in the confines of a 20-meter wide dressage arena is a new challenge for your ex-racer.

When bending correctly, the horse should remain on one track as he negotiates circles, corner, and turns. He should bend uniformly through his body and neck in the direction of travel and should not tip or tilt his head against the correct flexion.

When riding on a circle or through corners, your aids should be as follows:

Body position

Your outside hip and shoulder should be slightly forwards and your inside hip and shoulder slightly back.

Your seat should be parallel to the horse's shoulders

Rein aids

Guide the horse with both reins.

Keep your outside hand near the horse's neck with a firm, elastic contact to prevent him from falling out through his shoulder.

Open your inside hand towards the bend.

Keep your contact soft and relaxed so that you're not pulling the horse into the bend with your hand.

Leg aids

Use your inside leg on the girth to encourage the horse to bend around it, and keep your outside leg on as a passive aid to prevent the quarters from swinging out.

Hacking

Some riding horses are better at hacking than others, and it's the same with ex-racers.

Remember that although he has probably been out a lot, it will have always been in a string en-route to the gallops with lots of other horses. That's quite exciting! That said, most racehorses are more worldly than general riding horses, which can be helpful. However, you may find that some situations can cause the adrenalin to kick in and make life tricky for you.

Although most ex-racers are familiar with farm traffic, cars, dogs, etc., it really just depends on the individual horse and where his training yard was. Some of the major training enterprises are situated in relatively busy areas with lots of traffic, road markings, etc., whereas smaller operations in rural settings may have virtually no traffic and only quiet lanes surrounding them.

Some ex-racers will be less excitable alone, but pretty much all of them are more settled in pairs, rather than large groups. Groups of horses are too reminiscent of race days or riding to the gallops, and you'll most likely find that your horse gets "lit up" and excitable in that situation.

Ideally, you need a quiet, experienced horse to buddy-up with your ex-racer. Try to pick a circular ride that is as quiet as possible for your first adventure out. Make sure that you practice riding behind, alongside, and in front of the other horse. It's also a good idea to practice riding your horse away while his buddy stands still.

Be lavish with your praise whenever your horse is brave or well-behaved. You want your ex-racer to view hacking as a fun activity that's a part of his new career that he enjoys.

<u>A slight word of caution…</u>

In the beginning, avoid grassy tracks that look like gallops and wide-open spaces that could encourage your horse to expect to race. He's not naughty; he's merely doing what he's been trained to do, but a disaster here could be a major setback to the horse's re-training.

When you're confident that you have full control of your horse, go first and ask your hacking buddy to keep their distance so that your horse doesn't begin to race.

A note about galloping

We strongly advise you not to gallop your ex-racehorse, especially whilst you are re-training him.

Exercise riders and jockeys are professionals that gallop horses for a living; there is a skill to it.

Racehorses can reach speeds of 40mph (64kph) and if you do not know what you are doing the consequences could be severe to both you and your horse.

Galloping your horse at the same time as re-training him will also lead to a lot of confusion and could stop your horse from progressing. Remember that galloping requires the horse to balance on his forehand using his head and neck, which is exactly what we're trying to train him not to do.

If you eventually want to event your horse, then you will at some point need to gallop him for the cross-country phase. However, this is not recommended until you have a solid dressage foundation and partnership in place.

SECTION FOUR:

HOW TO TRAIN AN EX-RACEHORSE FOR DRESSAGE

THE TRAINING SCALES

At this point your ex-racehorse is being ridden regularly and understands basic aids. You're now ready to start dressage schooling work, but to do that you'll need to have a good understanding of the dressage training scale.

What are the German Scales of Training?

The six Scales of Training are what the riders in one of the world's most successful dressage nations are taught throughout their early years of riding.

The Scales are designed, through systematic training, to create an equine athlete who works in a perfect balance and makes the most of the movement they naturally possess.

The Scales of Training are:

1. Rhythm
2. Suppleness
3. Contact
4. Impulsion
5. Straightness
6. Collection

The Training Scales are meant to be approached in this order, although there are occasions when one can be skipped over in order to work on improving another, **there are no shortcuts!**

For your horse to achieve his maximum potential, it's crucial that you work methodically through the Scales, making steady progress.

The Scales are designed to link one to another

- Until your horse is working in **Rhythm**, he will not be able to become **Supple**.
- Until he is **Supple**, the **Contact** will be inconsistent.
- Until the **Contact** is established, **Impulsion** will not be true.
- If the horse is not working through a **Supple** back, forwards with **Impulsion** to a consistent, elastic **Contact**, he will not be **Straight**.
- In the early stages of the horse's training, **Collection** refers to balance. Only when a horse is established in the preceding five Scales will he be able to become sufficiently **Collected** (through the half-halt) to perform the advanced work that is demanded by the highest-level tests.

Why do you need to know this?

Well, training your horse along the Scales will ensure that he gradually becomes physically supple and strong enough to be able to do the work required at each level without sustaining injury.

Trying to take shortcuts can cause serious problems for your horse. For example, pulling the horse's head down into an "outline" will cause him to tighten and hollow his back, trail his hocks, and lose regularity in the rhythm. The horse will usually open his mouth against the contact, tilt his head, or drop behind the vertical to escape the rider's nagging hands. The end result of this scenario is a low mark for the test and a miserable horse with a sore mouth and back!

So, you can see from this example that a correctly trained horse is less likely to sustain long-term physical problems and will be much happier in his work. His dressage career is also likely to be longer than that of the horse whose rider has tried to take shortcuts and damaged their poor horse as a result!

Although achieving all these scales is your ultimate goal, The Training Scales are never truly completed, merely refined and refined. It is a never-ending quest to perfectionism.

Pre-requisite to the Scales of Training – Relaxation

Relaxation is a crucial element in dressage.

All the dressage Scales of Training are impacted negatively by tension. So, relaxation in both horse and rider are essential for good dressage.

In ex-racehorses, tension can be the enemy, so your first job is to persuade your horse to relax!

How you manage tension in your horse is largely down to your horse's individual personality. Some horses are more relaxed after they've been turned out or lunged. Whereas others become more settled and chilled out if given plenty of exercises to occupy their minds.

As you get to know your horse, you will find out what switches you need to flick to promote relaxation. If you have successfully and patiently completed steps 1-5 in the previous section, then this should be easier for you to achieve.

(There's more about solving the issue of tension on page 149.)

Training Scale #1 - Rhythm

Rhythm is the first and most important of all the training scales. If your horse does not work in the correct regular rhythm and appropriate tempo, you cannot hope to progress through the dressage levels successfully.

The quality of each individual horse's rhythm is determined by his natural paces. Most horses work in a clear rhythm naturally, whereas others can lose the purity of the gaits from time-to-time. Also, the rider can have a strong positive or negative influence on the horse's rhythm.

<u>The walk rhythm</u>

The rhythm in the walk should be clearly four-beat.

Sometimes, tension causes a horse to lose the clear four-beat rhythm, causing the legs on the same side to swing together, creating a lateral or pacing movement. That's a serious fault in a dressage horse and always receives a mark of 4 for each exercise in which the fault is present.

Often, if the horse is very tense, the medium walk becomes lateral, but as soon as the rider releases the contact in the free walk, the rhythm corrects itself as the horse relaxes.

A lateral walk will also earn a very poor score for paces in the collective marks, usually a 5.

You should be able to count out loud, one-two-three-four, one-two-three-four when the horse is walking. If you can't do that, the walk rhythm is most likely incorrect.

(More about correcting a lateral walk on page 160.)

The correct tempo for the walk will depend to some extent on the size of natural groundcover. A bigger walk will have a slower tempo. The easiest image of a correct tempo is encapsulated by the old hunting term, 'he looks like he's going home for lunch'. Another way to image it is to picture soldiers marching, purposeful and brisk, but unhurried.

The trot rhythm

The trot should have a two-beat rhythm so you will be able to count one-two, one-two, as the horse trots around the arena.

In the correct sequence at trot, the legs move in coordinated diagonal pairs with a clear moment of suspension between the two sets of footfalls.

Loss of rhythm in trot can be seen in either uneven height or uneven length of steps with one of more legs. If mild, this would be termed 'irregular' (length) or 'uneven' (height) and may be caused in odd moments by loss of balance, suppleness, or variations of impulsion or acceptance of the contact. When pronounced it indicates lameness.

Canter

The canter should have a three-time rhythm so you will be able to count, one-two-three, one-two-three, and tempo should be crisp but unhurried.

The correct sequence of legs in canter is;

- outside hind
- diagonal pair (inside hind and outside fore together)
- inside fore
- followed by a clear moment of suspension (all four feet off the ground)

The sequence then re-commences.

In right lead canter the right foreleg is the last footfall of the sequence, and vice versa for the left.

Incorrect 'cross cantering' or a 'disunited' canter comes about when the sequence is disrupted, and the pair of legs moving at the same moment are both on the same side.

In dressage horses, the canter can sometimes be four-beat. That occurs when the rider slows the canter too much and loses the impulsion and jump as a result.

When a horse is tense or very unbalanced, the rhythm can become two-time, and the pace becomes a mixture of the trot and canter (sometimes nicknamed a 'tranter').

Training Scale #2 - Suppleness

Once you have achieved a fair degree of rhythm (the first scale) in all the horse's paces, you can start to work on suppleness.

The British Dressage rule book defines suppleness as:

> *"The aim is that the horse's muscles have tone and are free from resistance, his joints are loose, and he does not tighten against the rider's aids. The muscles that are really important are those over the top line from the hind legs over the quarters, loins, in front of the wither and up to the poll.*
>
> *The test of whether a horse is supple and working 'through' the back and neck is that when the rein contact is eased (as in a free walk) the horse wants to stretch forward and down and not try to hollow and lift his head."*

As you can see, that description focuses mainly on longitudinal suppleness (over the back) but to fully understand suppleness we need to split it down into smaller chunks:

- Longitudinal suppleness – top line, to include back, neck, poll, and jaw
- Lateral suppleness – even and equal bend to the two sides

- Suppleness of the joints – essential for activity and ability to engage (weight carry)
- Mental suppleness – full acceptance of the aids, without any resistance

In practice, all of these areas are linked and as you work on one you will also improve the others.

Suppleness must be a central theme throughout schooling and should be constantly checked and reinforced at all stages. Just like rhythm, only if a horse is physically and mentally free from tension or constraint can he work with true suppleness and use himself fully. This mental aspect of suppleness should never be ignored.

Training Scale #3 - Contact

Ex-racers tend to find accepting an elastic contact to be extremely problematic. It's usually not the case that the horse is deliberately being resistant or difficult. Racehorses are trained to run through the bridle and go faster when the jockey picks up the rein contact. So, when you take up a contact and ask the horse to politely work into it, he simply doesn't understand.

Ex-racers typically carry their heads too high or too low, are very unsteady in the contact, and use the bridle for balance, especially in canter and through downward transitions.

Focusing on the contact can *only* be effective once the horse has the necessary rhythm and suppleness in his body to be able to maintain a steady connection through his back to the bit.

So, what defines the contact that you are looking for?

As a general guide:

- the horse should step forward to the contact, working through a supple poll
- the horse works over a raised and swinging back to allow the energy of the hindquarters to be transmitted into the bridle
- the horse accepts an elastic contact, quietly chewing the bit, without the tongue visible
- the poll is the highest point
- the nose should be slightly in front of the vertical, or on the vertical in higher degrees of collection
- in the medium and extended paces, the horse should visibly lengthen his entire frame, including his neck
- the outline is maintained without change when the rider gives the rein forward for a step or two, as in the movement described as 'give and retake'
- the horse seeks to take the contact forward and down when the rein is lengthened, for example in the free walk

When re-training your ex-racer, remember that the ideal that's detailed above is the perfect contact scenario that you're working toward and it's not something that's going to happen overnight. It is achieved through systematically training the rhythm and suppleness elements of the Scales of Training.

Training Scale #4 - Impulsion

Impulsion is defined by the FEI as:

> *"The transmission of controlled, propulsive energy generated from the hindquarters into the athletic movement of the eager horse. Its ultimate expression can be shown only through the horse's soft and swinging back and is guided by the gentle contact with the rider's hand."*

So, from that you can see that creating impulsion is dependent on rhythm, suppleness, and contact (the first three training scales), and these are essential for the control and direction of impulsion.

Ex-racers tend to fall into two categories when it comes to impulsion:

1. Too much impulsion

Sometimes the horse will run away from the leg through tension, overexcitement, lack of balance, or not understanding the rider's leg aids. That can cause the horse to lose rhythm, increase tempo, tighten through his back, shorten his neck, become unsteady in the contact, or all of the above!

2. Not enough impulsion

Impulsion and speed are not the same thing.

Some ex-racehorses lack impulsion because they are not working in front of the leg correctly. That results in flat, un-elastic paces, a slow response to the rider's aids, difficulties with lateral work, and obvious aids required just to keep the horse going.

What's required to achieve impulsion?

Aside from the previous scales already mentioned, other pre-requisites for impulsion are:

- reasonable balance
- freedom from tension
- understanding of both the driving aids and the controlling aids
- lack of resistance anywhere in the body or mind
- forward-thinking (FORWARD is an attitude of mind, not speed)
- elastic movement of the limbs
- active hind leg with vigorous bending of the joints

- a 'quick' hind leg, which does not trail out behind the body, but picks up ready to move forward again at (or only just past) the point where the hock moves behind the point of the buttocks
- hind legs that step forward under the center of gravity
- the ability to over-track

That's quite a shopping list for an ex-racer that's new to dressage training. However, you can achieve all those things through patient, correct and systematic training.

Training Scale #5 - Straightness

Straightness is probably the most difficult of the scales to place in terms of order.

Although it is fifth on the scale, it is quite integral to achieving the earlier scales. In other words, the scales are all inter-related, and this is the most obvious example.

Sound complicated? Try to think of straightness in the following terms to gain a better understanding.

1. 'Straightness' is rather a misnomer, a better word to use is 'alignment'.
2. The forefeet must be aligned with the hind feet on straight and curved lines.
3. The horse should have equal bend (and hence, alignment) on both reins.

So, you can see that this sounds a lot like the second item on the scales, suppleness. It is also integral to gaining equal contact in both hands, and developing impulsion, which depends on both hind legs thrusting with equal power and in the same direction.

All horses are born crooked and straightening them is a never-ending task; without monitoring, their natural crookedness will reassert itself.

Through developing even weight distribution on both sides of the horse, you are helping him to maintain health and soundness for ridden work, by promoting equal wear on the muscles, tendons, joints, and ligaments of both sides.

Racehorse are predominantly worked on the left rein, so although straightness may not be a priority in the earlier stages, you'll need to start paying attention to it from the word go. Straightening natural crookedness takes months and years of persistent work, and although you may not *achieve* it until the horse is relatively advanced in training terms, you will need to work on it as an underlying issue pretty much as soon as your basic controls are established.

Training Scale #6 - Collection

Collection is the last of the training scales and is dependent on a fair degree of accomplishment of the earlier scales, i.e. rhythm, suppleness, contact, impulsion, and straightness. If there are any missing links in the earlier stages, achieving true collection will not be possible.

In a nutshell, collection is the re-balancing of the horse carrying the foreign weight of the rider teaching him to carry more of the (combined) weight on his hind quarters than on his shoulders. This makes him more balanced and able to perform ridden movements with ease and in a beautiful and biomechanically functional carriage that gives the appearance of traveling uphill.

Insufficient collection results in a loss of submission, because the horse is not able to perform the movements with ease and fluency.

Collection refers to differences in:

- Stride length (shorter)
- Stride height (taller)
- Overall balance – with more weight clearly distributed to the hindquarters rather than the shoulders
- A shorter, taller outline as a result of the above change in weight distribution (i.e., *not* because you've just shortened the reins and pulled the neck higher).

So don't try to cram your horse together between stronger hands and legs to find shorter steps – that's NOT what collection is about; it is the gradual development of the ability and strength to carry more weight behind and less on the shoulders, with the above differences as a *consequence* of collection, and not the other way around.

Degrees of collection

There are several degrees of collection, as appropriate to each stage of the horse's training.

First-degree collection

First-degree collection is what you'll observe in a young horse.

Transitions are usually progressive, rather than direct, allowing the horse to keep his balance. Halts may not be completely square behind, and that's acceptable for a horse at the beginning of his dressage career.

Second-degree collection

A horse who is working with second-degree collection will be able to make direct transitions and show a degree of collection and shortening throughout his whole body.

Third-degree collection

A horse with third-degree collection should carry at least half his bodyweight on his hindquarters. The horse's carriage will be more uphill, transitions will be smoother and more fluent, and the horse will appear light on his feet.

Horses working with third-degree collection can show the beginnings of piaffe and passage.

Fourth-degree collection

Fourth-degree collection is the most advanced level of collection and is seen in horses working at Grand Prix level.

Collection and balance

In terms of training your ex-racer in the early days, collection refers mainly to balance.

The degree of collection required at a specific level is only so much as to be able to perform the required movement with ease. So, at the lower levels when collection is first introduced, that's not much.

All the judge is looking for is that the horse can bring his weight enough off his shoulders to be able to, for example, perform a 10-meter circle without struggling, or make a downward transition from canter to walk (as in a simple change) without pitching forward and putting all his weight onto either his front feet or the reins.

As you progress further up the levels, you should be able to produce a little more collection – enough to show movements like shoulder in, half pass, and travers with reasonable ease and engagement. The higher the level, the higher the degree of collection required, until at the top levels you have enough to produce, for example, a canter pirouette in balance and with visible ease.

Through systematic training, you can teach your horse to take more weight onto his hindquarters, which in turn will lift his forehand, help to balance him through transitions, and enable him to negotiate small circles more easily.

FIRST SCHOOLING EXERCISES

At this point, your horse should have settled into his new exercise routine, and although his ridden work may be a bit rough, you are able to ride him on both reins and in all three paces.

In the previous chapter, we talked all about The Training Scales, so in this chapter we're going to look at some useful schooling exercises that you can use to develop the requirements of the training scales and improve your horse's overall way of going.

Notes before you begin

- You can do the following exercises in any order and even combine a few of them together to increase the difficulty.
- When introducing a new exercise or movement, start on the rein that the horse finds the easiest. Once the 'penny has dropped' you can then ride it on the other rein.
- These are general exercises and movements that you can introduce into your horse's schooling. For exercises to help you fix specific problems, check out the next chapter.

Exercise #1 – Downward transitions

A well-ridden downward transition shortens the horse's frame, makes him more engaged, and encourages him to take more weight onto his hind legs. The haunches are lowered, making the horse's balance more uphill and lightening the forehand.

So, instead of falling in a heap, the horse transitions smoothly from one pace to another, maintaining his rhythm and balance.

Here's how to ride a downward transition:

Step 1

Use your seat and legs.

Sit tall in the deepest part of the saddle. Stretch your legs down and close them around the horse's barrel. That engages the horse hindquarters and brings them more underneath him.

Step 2

Use your reins.

Without pulling back on the reins, close your hand. That has the effect of restraining the horse's forehand, preventing him from moving forward from your leg.

As soon as the horse makes the downward transition, soften the rein, and allow him to move forward again.

How does a good downward transition feel?

A good downward transition should feel smooth, not bumpy and rough, and the horse should feel light in your hands.

Rather than feeling as though you are falling off a cliff, the horse's shoulders should lift, and you should feel as though you are both moving up a hill.

Exercise #2 – Upward transitions

When judging upward transitions, the judge is looking for obedience, responsiveness, and harmony.

The transition should be sharp but not rushed, the horse should maintain his frame, and the balance must be uphill as it was in the downward transitions.

Here's how to ride an upward transition:

Step 1

Use your leg and seat.

Keeping a supple seat within the rhythm of the pace, increase the pressure of your leg slightly to encourage the horse to go forward.

Step 2

Use your reins.

The rein aid tells the horse that it's not time to "go" just yet. As you feel the energy increase beneath you, ease your inside rein to allow the horse to make the upward transition with plenty of energy. Keep the outside rein contact to prevent the horse from falling out through his shoulder as he makes the transition.

Note that the rhythm and tempo should remain the same throughout the transition.

How does a good upward transition feel?

You should feel your horse's back lifting underneath you as he pushes himself forward with his hind legs, steps underneath his body, and his center of gravity changes.

The overall impression is of a powerboat; the prow of the boat rises, and the stern powers the craft forward.

Exercise #3 – Square halts

In a good halt, the horse should be straight and square. Each leg should bear the same weight evenly so that the horse has 'a leg at each corner'.

Regardless of the pace you are approaching the halt from, it's important to 'think forward' when riding into the transition. If you just close the reins and fail to use enough leg, the horse will lose engagement as he halts. The halt will become unbalanced, and he will probably not be square behind.

Step 1

As you prepare to halt, help your horse by riding two or three shorter, more collected trot or walk steps in the approach to the transition, while keeping the horse moving forward. That will push the horse's hind legs underneath him, helping him to maintain his balance and giving him every chance of halting square.

Give your horse a clear half-halt, and cease following the movement with your seat, but be careful not to ride too abruptly into halt as that will only serve to unbalance your horse, and he will probably not halt square.

Step 2

Close your hand and leg.

Don't simply pull backwards on the reins, instead, use a 'forward' hand. That will keep your horse soft, round, and stepping underneath with his hind legs so that he doesn't lean on your hand for balance in the transition itself.

Keep both legs on and maintain an even contact in both reins to make sure the horse stays straight.

Step 3

Don't be tempted to "fiddle" with the halt too much. That's a mistake that many riders make. You can make minor adjustments but once the halt is established, sit still and allow the horse to relax and mouth quietly on the bit.

Step 4

When the horse has achieved a good, square, straight halt and has waited obediently for your next instruction, always make a big fuss of him. It's just as important to reward your horse when he gets it right as it is to correct him.

When you're happy with the halt, ask the horse to walk on (or proceed in whatever pace is required).

Exercise #4 – Circles

Circles are designed to test the horse's balance, suppleness to the bend, and straightness, and as such, should form a major part of your schooling program at home.

To help position your circle accurately and keep it round, think of riding a diamond shape where each point of the diamond touches the quarter point of the circle. Now ride the diamond and round-off each point.

The aids for riding a circle

Your horse should continue to work forwards, in a good rhythm and showing a clear uniform bend along his body around the circle.

The smaller the circle, the more bend the horse must show.

- your inside leg on the girth keeps the impulsion, develops the engagement of the inside hind leg, and asks for bend
- your outside leg slightly behind the girth prevents the hindquarters from escaping to the outside of the circle and generates some forward movement
- your inside hand asks for some bend through the horse's neck
- your outside hand controls the pace and prevents too much neck bend which would allow the horse to drift out through his shoulder
- keep your hips and shoulders parallel with your horse's shoulders, keep your body upright, and look ahead of you around the circle

When practicing smaller circles, it can be helpful to position cones or buckets in your arena at home to mark out where each 'point' of your circle should be. This will show you just how supple your horse really is and helps you to be more accurate.

Exercise #5 – Figure of eight

The figure of eight exercise is designed to develop the horse's suppleness to the bend, to make him straighter, and to improve his balance. It's also used in dressage tests as a test of accuracy and to allow the judge to assess the effectiveness and correctness of the rider's outside aids.

Step 1

Begin by riding a 20-meter circle from A.

Bend your horse around your inside leg, asking for a small amount of inside flexion through his neck and poll with your inside rein.

Keep your outside leg slightly behind the girth to prevent the quarters from escaping and maintain an elastic guarding contact with your outside rein to keep your horse straight.

Step 2

As you approach X, make your horse straight for a couple of strides.

If you are in rising trot, change your diagonal here.

Now change the bend before commencing a half 20-meter circle around the opposite end of the arena to finish at C.

Step 3

From C, continue around the second half of the 20-meter circle, maintaining the new bend until you arrive back at X.

Over X, make your horse straight for a couple of strides, before changing the bend again and riding another 20-meter half-circle around to A.

Exercise #6 – Trot-walk-trot transition

The trot-walk-trot exercise help to tune your horse into your aids and is an exercise that is included in dressage tests at the lower levels.

Step 1

First of all, make sure that your horse is in a good, active trot, working nicely forward from behind through his back into a secure, elastic contact.

Look ahead towards the point where you want to make the transitions and remember to give your horse a clear half-halt before you get there so that he is prepared.

Step 2

Go into sitting trot a few strides before you ask for the transition into walk, and don't allow the horse to slow down to a jog.

Keep your leg on as the horse makes the transition and ride forward so that the horse's inside hind leg steps through and underneath to balance him. Remember that if you allow your horse to dawdle into the walk transition, he's more likely to drift sideways and loose straightness.

Step 3

Keep the walk steps active. Plenty of activity in the walk means that you will achieve a better upward transition back into trot. In addition, the more engaged the horse is the more uphill his balance will be as he makes the transition.

Step 4

Ask the horse to trot forward.

The transition back into trot should be obedient and reactive, whilst remaining fluent and calm. The horse should remain in the same outline throughout the whole exercise, and the trot rhythm and energy following the transition should be the same as it was prior to the walk steps.

Exercise #7 – Serpentines

A serpentine is basically a series of half circles that form 'S' shaped loops across the arena.

Serpentines are extremely good exercises for suppling your horse around your inside leg and for helping to develop rider coordination and timing. The changes of direction and bend make this an exercise that is particularly useful for keeping the attention of a horse that is easily distracted or who is inclined to switch off during routine schooling sessions. If your horse tends to hurry and lose rhythm and balance, riding serpentines can also help to steady the tempo and put him back on an even keel.

As a schooling exercise, the serpentine is very versatile. For example, you could ride serpentines in walk, trot or canter with different numbers of loops and include transitions over the center line if you wanted to.

Step 1

Begin riding the serpentine in the middle of one short side of the arena (at either A or C).

To create the first loop, ride a half circle, making sure that your horse is bent around your inside leg and is stepping forward into a softly supporting outside rein so that he does not drift out through his shoulder.

Your inside rein should not be used to pull the horse around the half circle, but rather to create a small amount of flexion to the bend.

Keep your outside leg on the horse, slightly behind the girth to control the quarters and to stop them from swinging out.

Step 2

Straighten your horse across the middle of the school, so that he is parallel to the short side for approximately one horse's length.

Now, give your horse a half-halt to balance him and reverse your aids to change the bend.

If you're riding the exercise in trot, don't forget to change your diagonal.

Ride a second half-circle and repeat.

TIP: Make sure that you don't ride your loops right into the corners of the arena – they are meant to be half circles, not square corners!

Exercise #8 – 5-meter loops

A 5-meter loop is a shallow serpentine and is a very suitable figure to ride during warm up as it demands changes of bend without too extreme a change of direction, so minimizing the likelihood of loss of balance or alignment to the figure (straightness).

The exercise should be a series of gradual curves, not a straight line to a sharp turn.

Let's take an example of riding on the left rein, a loop between F and M.

Step 1

Begin the movement by riding off the track directly from F – do not allow your horse to cling to the track and drift past the marker; you should be leaving the track by the time your own body passes F.

Make the turn by turning your torso to the left a bit more than you did during the preceding corner and putting a little more weight into your left stirrup.

The turn of your upper body will have brought your left (inside) hand slightly away from his shoulder to lead him inward, and your right (outside) hand inward and forward, to control the shoulder while allowing the bend.

Step 2

Aim at a point just a couple of meters before your midpoint, which is 5-meters in from B (on the quarter line, halfway between B and X).

About halfway between leaving the track and arriving at this midpoint, change your diagonal and begin to change your horse's bend until he arrives at the quarter line already in a *right* bend and performing a gentle right-hand curve at the peak of your loop. Ask for this by reversing your upper body position so it is now turning towards the right, and your weight is slightly more in your right stirrup.

<u>Step 3</u>

As you arrive at the halfway point between the peak of the loop and your end goal (M), change your diagonal again and once more reverse your body position – shoulders turning left and weight in the left stirrup, so that you arrive at M in left bend, all ready to travel around the next corner.

Exercise #9 – Leg-yield

Leg yield is a great exercise for increasing suppleness and engagement and for placing the horse securely into your outside rein.

1. Begin by walking down the three-quarter line of the school. As your horse walks forward, use your inside leg on the girth to ask him to step sideways away from your inside leg back towards the track. If necessary, 'lead' him with your outside rein.

2. Ask for a very small amount of inside flexion at the horse's poll, whilst keeping the rest of his body straight. The horse should remain almost parallel to the fence with his forehand slightly in advance of the hindquarters.

You can also combine this with Exercise #11 and ride it on a circle; leg yielding the horse away from the center of the circle, then back in again.

Exercise #10 – Shoulder-in

Shoulder-in is an exercise that is performed on three tracks and would normally follow on in the horse's education after the leg yielding.

It can be ridden in walk, trot, and canter and is an excellent suppling and engaging exercise through which the horse will learn to flex and bend, and shorten and heighten the steps.

- The horse should have a slight but even bend around the rider's inside leg to create an angle of about 30 degrees.
- The horse's outside foreleg and inside hindleg should work on the same track. The inside foreleg and the outside hindleg should work on their own track.
- The horse should have bend away from the direction in which he is moving.

Its purpose is to enable the hind legs to step under and elevate the forehand.

The exercise also mobilizes and frees the shoulders, which enables the rider to place the forehand and engage the hind legs, thus building collection and compression in the way of going.

Shoulder-in is an effective straightening tool, in both trot and canter, and can be ridden on lines next to the arena boundary or on unsupported lines in the middle of the arena, for example on the center line.

<u>Riding shoulder-in</u>

Providing that the horse has been well prepared in the leg yielding steps, controlling the placement of the shoulders should not be too difficult.

Ideally, start on short straight lines next to the arena fence out of a well-ridden corner or off a small circle.

When riding shoulder-in to the left, the horse is bent around the rider's left leg and the outside (right) leg is just behind the girth.

The left leg moves the horse sideways; the expansion of the horse's right (outside) is supported by the rider's right leg and right rein which subtly leads the horse in the direction of the movement.

The rider's inside leg and seat need to make the horse react quickly and also step up into the inside rein.

The rider's outside leg is responsible for keeping the engagement of the right hind leg forwards and under the body weight. This then encourages the horse to bring the inside hind further under the body, thus developing engaging hind legs.

The horse's croup will lower, and his shoulders will become freer to allow the forehand to elevate.

The rider's shoulders and hips should be parallel to those of the horse.

It is advisable to keep the initial distances short, so as not to let the horse become out of balance and hence more onto the shoulders. Even at the start, the horse must be inclined to step under with the hind legs and take more of his own body weight.

Exercise #11 – Spirals

Spiraling in and out of a 20-meter circle is a really simple way of increasing the engagement of the horse's hindquarters, thereby improving both his balance and his suppleness.

1. Before you start, place a cone or some other marker where you want the center of your circle to be. Ride a 20-meter circle, keeping the cone as the center point.

2. Gradually spiral in to decrease the size of the circle. Think of the circle as a bull's-eye and make your circle one ring smaller on each revolution.

3. Keep the rhythm and impulsion whilst spiraling in, using your inside leg to your outside rein. When you reach the smallest circle your horse can comfortably manage, spiral back out again.

The exercise works by allowing the horse to gradually adjust his bend and balance to cope with the increased demands of a smaller circle. In order to maintain the rhythm, impulsion and bend, he increases the flexion and engagement of his hocks.

Exercise #12 – Bend and counter-bend (on a circle)

Asking the horse to 'counter-bend' is a simple and effective exercise for improving suppleness and balance. Counter-bend simply means asking the horse to bend in the opposite direction to that in which he is turning. In other words, if you're riding a circle to the right, your horse would be bent to the left.

1. Start in walk on the right rein and introduce the exercise around the short side of the school, before attempting to do it on a circle.

2. Open your left rein, keep your left leg on the girth, and ask the horse to bend around it. Your left leg is pushing your horse's shoulder around the turns, while your right hand should lead him. Turn your upper body and head in the direction of the turn to help the horse understand that he needs to turn right, even though he's bent to the

left.

3. Remember to include plenty of changes of rein, and keep your horse moving forward.

Exercise #13 – Half-halts

You can use the half-halt to put your horse 'on the bit', to prepare for changes of pace, to balance your horse, and to set your horse up for lateral exercises.

The word 'halt' can be misleading. Riders often override the half-halt and kill the impulsion that is so important. Instead, think of the half-halt as more of a 'half-go', and use the aid to gather together all the energy that your leg and seat have created.

To give a connecting half-halt, you'll use three sets of aids:

- seat and both legs (driving aids)
- inside rein and both legs (bending aids)
- the rein of opposition (outside rein)

<u>Step 1</u>

First of all, close both your calves around your horse and squeeze him to create a surge of power from his hindquarters. As you ask for more power, cease following the horse's movement with your seat, as if you were about to ride a downward transition. This helps to shift the horse's balance back onto his hind legs.

<u>Step 2</u>

Next, close your outside hand into a fist. This captures, contains, and recycles the energy back to the hind legs to bring them more underneath the horse.

Step 3

Finally, squeeze and release the inside rein to keep the horse's neck straight. This is important in order to prevent too much outside bend while you're applying the rein of opposition.

Step 4

The whole exercise lasts for only one stride. Once you've given the half-halt, go back to your original light contact and maintenance leg pressure, and ride the horse forwards.

FIXING COMMON PROBLEMS

Ex-racers are not blank canvases. They are equine athletes that have been trained with an extremely specific skill set. So, rather than starting from scratch, your job is to teach the horse to respond to a different set of aids, to develop muscles and suppleness in areas of his body that he wouldn't use in his normal daily work as a racehorse. Also, the horse has to learn how to carry a (most likely) heavier rider who sits in a completely different position to that of his jockey!

On that journey, that you're more than likely going to run into a few problems that are common when it comes to re-training ex-racehorses. To help you out, we have listed several of them below, together with a few solutions.

Problem #1 - Rushing

Although it is desirable and indeed necessary for a dressage horse to work forwards from the rider's leg, problems can arise when the horse is in too much of a hurry! This can lead to the tempo of the rhythm becoming too quick and the purity of the paces being lost. Further issues then arise with loss of balance, especially through transitions and around turns.

The rider must learn to keep the horse's legs slow and under control until the horse begins to relax.

Contrary to instinct, the rider **should not** take the legs away from the horse's side. Even if the horse is anxious, wanting to run away and hollow, the rider must be coordinated enough to leave their legs in a 'breathable' contact next to the horse's ribs.

The horse should learn to breathe into the rider's lower legs and slow down; equally, the rider must choose an appropriate slower tempo.

This exercise helps to teach your horse to accept your leg without rushing.

<u>Not rushing in walk</u>

Start by riding a 20-meter circle in a walk, keeping a constant, quiet leg contact. Try to keep your legs still, using just enough pressure to prevent them from moving away from your horse's sides.

Your horse should stay relaxed. If he tries to rush off, don't allow him to pull you forward out of the saddle. Sit straight and deep. Keep your leg on quietly and ask the horse to walk with a steady elastic rein contact.

Repeat the exercise until the horse is calm and doesn't try to hurry or become strong.

If you keep your aids and your position consistent and steady, your horse will learn what to expect from you, and he won't associate your leg contact with rushing forward.

<u>Not rushing in trot</u>

Now that your horse is settled and accepting your legs at a walk, quietly ask him to trot, still on your 20-meter circle. Use a small push with your seat to ask for the trot, keeping your legs passive against the horse's sides and maintaining a consistent, elastic contact with your horse's mouth.

Take up a rising trot and keep the tempo steady. As you rise, count out the "one-two" rhythm in your head so that you can tell if he begins to speed up. If your horse starts to hurry, keep your leg on quietly, sit to the trot, and ask him to walk, holding your position and keeping your rein contact steady.

Repeat the exercise, using very quiet aids. As soon as the horse starts to rush, bring him back to walk.

Throughout the exercise, keep your leg steadily on the horse, keep a consistent contact with his mouth, and maintain an even tempo. Once the horse stops trying to rush, move off your circle, add in some serpentines, and use the whole arena. The moment the horse speeds up, go back to your 20-meter circle and repeat the exercise.

<u>Venturing into canter</u>

When the walk and trot are calm and steady, try the canter. The canter is usually where the "wheels come off" when re-training an ex-racer.

Start on your 20-meter circle and ask for a transition into canter followed by a few steps. As soon as the horse begins to quicken, bring him back to trot.

Repeat the exercise, gradually increasing the number of canter steps until you can negotiate a whole circle without the horse rushing.

Throughout these exercises maintain your position and don't allow the horse to pull you forward.

Problem #2 - Leaning on the bit/heavy in the hand

Leaning on the bit is the common description for any horse that puts an undue amount of his own weight on the bit whilst being ridden. A horse that leans on the bit will typically cause his rider quite a bit of muscle strain and discomfort because the horse is using the rider as a means of support and balance.

Leaning on the bit is a bad habit that takes time, conditioning, and a certain amount of rider experience to correct.

In order to stop your horse from leaning on the bit, you'll need to teach him to become more engaged and to carry himself without using your hands for balance. He will need to lighten his forehand and learn to seek a lighter contact.

When re-training a horse not to lean on your hands, a good starting point is to use transitions. Ride transitions from one pace to another and within the paces too. Using circles whilst riding transitions can help to bring the horse's inside hind leg more underneath him, which will, in turn, lift his forehand and relieve his reliance for balance on your contact.

Lateral work such as leg-yielding and shoulder-in can be useful in developing the horse's engagement and encouraging him to lighten his forehand. You can practice incorporating shoulder-in and leg-yield whilst riding circles to really drive the horse's hind leg underneath and therefore lighten his shoulders.

Make sure that you ride forwards through both upward and downward transitions so that the horse does not 'dwell' on the hand and has to use his hindquarters more efficiently.

Remember that faults such as this cannot be fixed overnight. Patience, practice and time will eventually pay dividends.

Problem #3 – Tension

Relaxation in dressage is crucial. If the horse is tense, several negative things happen:

- the rhythm will become inconsistent or irregular
- the horse will become tight through his topline
- the contact will become unsteady
- the horse will come against the rider's hand or duck behind the

bridle
- the tempo may become too quick or inconsistent
- the horse will stiffen against the rider's aids to bend
- the horse may become crooked
- transitions will be unbalanced and rough
- harmony between horse and rider will be lost

Rider tension

When the rider is tense, the horse becomes tight through his muscles, ligaments, and joints. Tension in the rider manifests itself through:

- Gripping the reins too tightly
- Tension in the buttocks, creating a bounce in the saddle
- Locked hips that don't follow the horse's movement
- A clenched jaw
- Knees gripping the saddle, pushing the seat upward and away from the horse

If any part of your body is tense and tight, that will affect other parts of you too. And when you are tense, your mount will reflect that tension back at you. So, the first thing you need to do is ensure that you are relaxed, confident, and in control of your own nerves.

Horse tension

Tense horses are usually very tight through their topline. Lateral work can be extremely effective in encouraging mental and physical relaxation in a tense horse.

Exercise #1 - Spiral on a circle

Moving the horse in and out of a circle is a highly effective way of teaching him to accept your leg. The exercise can be ridden in canter and trot, depending on what works best for your horse.

1. Ride a 20-meter circle in trot or canter.
2. Use your outside leg to push the horse onto a circle of 18-meters. Now, use your inside leg to move the horse back out onto a 20-meter circle.
3. If the horse tries to go faster or tightens up, make the circle smaller to control the tempo.

If your horse is unbalanced and tends to break the canter, ride the exercise in trot. Making the exercise easier for the horse will help to reduce tension and anxiety.

Exercise #2 - Leg-yield on the diagonal line

When you can safely apply your leg without an explosion, you can work on teaching your horse to listen to the leg aid.

- In working trot, ride leg-yield from the corner of the arena, across the diagonal line.
- As you approach the end of the diagonal, ride a few steps of medium trot.
- Focus on keeping the rhythm and tempo of the trot consistent. The horse must learn not to go faster but to relax and take bigger steps to cover more ground.

Exercise #3 - Head-to-the-wall leg-yield

1. In working trot, ride down the long side of the arena. Turn your horse's head to the fence, and ride leg-yield with your horse's shoulders on the fence and his quarters to the inside. You don't need any bend in the horse's body, and there should be no outside

flexion. Ideally, the horse should move on three or four tracks.
2. Make the horse straight before you reach the corner.

The fence acts as an extra brake, preventing the horse from running away from you. As you apply more leg to drive him forward and sideways, the horse's sideways steps should become bigger.

The exercise works because the crossing of the hind legs loosens and lifts the horse's back, removing tightness and tension.

Exercise #4 - Leg-yield on a circle

The previous exercise can also be ridden on a circle.

1. Picture your horse as a carousel horse with the pole running through his belly button.
2. Now, place that pole on the line of the circle. Keep the horse's body straight with his shoulders to the inside of the line and his quarters to the outside.
3. Keep the circle at 20-meters, and don't allow the horse to fall in to decrease the angle that you're asking him for.

It's crucial that you keep the tempo consistent. The horse should gradually increase his length of stride without hurrying or getting faster.

Other exercises

Useful exercises to retrain the anxious horse include:

- lots of walking and up and down hills
- simple turns and shapes incorporating many walk-halt exercises
- walk-trot and trot-walk transitions
- turns about the haunches and forehand to raise the shoulders and back

- lungeing using side reins
- bending using serpentines, loops, and figures

These exercises are useful and help the horse starts to build trust and confidence in the rider.

Other relaxation tips

Every horse is different, and different things can trigger tension in individuals. Here are some management factors to consider if you keep facing tension in your ridden work.

- Provide the horse with more time turned out in the field
- Exercise the horse twice a day (e.g. morning hack and afternoon schooling session)
- Provide table toys to help keep the horse's brain occupied
- Provide equine company to help keep the horse relaxed

Problem #4 – Snatching at the reins

When trying to stop your horse from snatching at the reins, the most suitable course of action firstly involves keeping calm, and secondly, analyzing exactly in what type of situation the habit manifests itself.

For example, some horses may snatch the reins in the following situations:

- at the very start of exercise
- having just been mounted at a competition
- mid-session after training an area of weakness, e.g. transitions
- end of a training session if the horse is particularly fatigued
- in an unusually tense environment, e.g. warm-up at a competition
- in a gait of a slower tempo, e.g. medium or free walk in a dressage test

- in moments of relaxation between movements in a session
- young horses that are mentally and physically tired

Snatching the reins is usually a sign of tension or anxiety. The horse may be generally working quite well and showing daily signs of progression in the training exercises and just momentarily snatches the reins in a quiet moment. This is not unusual and certainly does not warrant a reprimand.

If the rider recognizes snatching in any of the above situations, that is a positive start!

If the snatching occurs predominantly after a strenuous part of an exercise, this is fairly easily dealt with. Here are some tips.

Tip #1

Make sure that your leg and rein aids get a prompt response. If the horse needs lots of repetitive leg aids for one simple exercise, the repetition of 'weak' aids may cause anxiety.

This is the best way to sort out the problem – looking to the aids!

Tip #2

Identify how supple the horse is. Any stiffening that causes resistance to the bend or staying in a together, working frame, can cause unnecessary tension and/or hollowing, which is usually a precursor to snatching.

Tip #3

Intend to work the horse into a consistent rein and seat contact to enable the horse to build up good musculature in the hindquarters and back. This is a principle that will help the horse to carry himself more on the hind legs. This means that he will be less likely to 'tip' onto the riders' hands, potentially a cause of snatching.

<u>Tip #4</u>

In the early stages of the horse's re-training, allow the horse frequent walk breaks, even in a short session. This will enable the musculature to build up in the recovery state and help prevent stress and fatigue.

<u>Tip #5</u>

Try not to keep the horse in the same tempo or frame for too long. All horses need frequent variations of tempo and frequent moments in which to stretch the top line muscles so that they do not become tired and inflexible.

This is especially true in the early stages of your horse's re-training. Remember that if the horse feels 'fixed' or rigid, this will cause mental anxiety and predispose to snatching as a learned behavior, which is much more difficult to eradicate.

<u>Tip #6</u>

Give rewards during exercise either by patting the neck, touching the withers with the index finger mid-exercise, and/or using the voice in an appropriate and rewarding tone. This will help keep the horse with you and prevent nervousness, anxiety and/or tension.

Problem #5 – Standing still

An important element of the halt exercise is 'immobility'. Immobility means that your horse should remain perfectly still, whilst remaining on your aids.

Learning to stand still is also important if you include hacking out in your horse's exercise program. The last thing you want when waiting at a junction to cross a busy road is for your horse to be hopping about on the spot or sidling over the white lines!

Like every exercise you perform, immobility requires practice. Standing still should be made part of your daily work routine. So, after every transition to halt, make sure your horse stands still for a few seconds before moving off. This will get your horse into the habit of remaining immobile whilst waiting for your next aid, instead of just barging off regardless of his rider!

Use your voice to praise and relax your horse as he stands.

Don't get into an argument with the contact; if the horse ignores your hand and tries to barge off, quietly insist that he stands still, but if necessary, walk forwards, soften him into the contact, and begin again.

Although some horses are just natural fidgets, a balanced halt is very important in establishing immobility. If the horse is not standing square with his weight evenly distributed over all four legs, he will be more inclined to step sideways or backwards in an effort to balance himself and his rider. However, if your horse habitually halts with a hind leg trailing, make sure you've trained him to stand still before you begin to tackle the issue of the square halt. If you always move your horse in an effort to square-up the halt before he's actually standing still, you're in danger of training him to fidget every time you ask him to stand.

Once the horse is standing square, establish at least three seconds of immobility before you ask him to move off. Make sure that the horse walks forward in response to your aids, not just because he thinks he can!

It's a good idea to practice halting in different parts of the arena as the last thing you want is for your horse to anticipate halting, especially as you'll need him to be working forward in order to maintain his engagement and balance as you ride into the halt.

Finally, always finish each training session with a good halt and insist on immobility before you dismount. There's nothing worse than a horse that's half-way across the arena and heading for his stable before you've even taken your feet out of the stirrups!

Problem #6 – Spooking

As prey animals, it is only natural that the horse's survival instincts have given him an incredible ability to jerk all his muscles in an instantaneous response to a potential threat.

Spooking has many different causes. However, whether it is inexperience, legitimate fear, intentionally naughty behavior, or just a chronic ability to see ghosts where there are none, spooking is an irritating habit!

Whatever the reason, there is no benefit to using punishment or losing your temper with the spooky horse. This only reinforces the horse's initial flight response and can make the habit worse.

<u>Tips to help conquer spooking</u>

If the scary object is at one end of the school, circle in the center. As your horse relaxes, gradually work your circle inwards toward the scary end of the school.

This slow way of dealing with spooking usually ends up getting the fastest results, and you can achieve your goal with a minimum of resistance and trauma to your horse and to you.

When you're at least 15 meters from the scary object, use your inside rein to gently but firmly bend your horse's neck enough to the inside, so he can't see it with either eye. Remember, a horse has both binocular vision (like a human), and monocular vision where he can see with each eye separately. So, you need to bend the neck enough so he can't see the object with either eye. He won't shy from what he can't see.

Once you are directly beside the scary object, relax both reins. Many horses are claustrophobic, and you don't want your horse to think he's being forced against something with no escape.

Breathe! If you're holding your breath, you'll convince your horse there's a good reason to be afraid. Inhale deeply and, as you exhale feel your bottom lowering down into the saddle.

If your horse begins to shy away from something in the dressage arena, try positioning him in shoulder-in as you approach it and ride him forwards. This positioning will make it difficult for the horse to focus on the scary object as he won't be able to see it, and he will find it physically difficult to spook away too.

Look up and ahead to where you want to be, not down at the tiger as you ride past.

Here are some don'ts to bear in mind when riding the spooky horse.

- **Don't** punish a spooky horse. Shying comes from fear. If you punish your horse for shying, you convince him he was right to be afraid in the first place!
- **Don't** soothe your horse by patting him while he's shying. This action just rewards the behavior you don't want.
- **Don't** make a nervous horse walk straight up to something scary. That's the most frightening thing you can do to a flight animal. It's effectively like asking a horse to come face to face with the tiger at 'B', when every instinct tells him to run from danger.
- **Don't** stare at the scary object. If you focus on it, your horse will too. Look up and ahead of the hazard instead.

Problem #7 – Behind the vertical

Sometimes, for various reasons, your horse may curl up behind the contact, which is also described as being 'behind the vertical'.

More often than not, horses that come easily behind the contact are quite light in the mouth. By staying behind the contact they can make the bit lighter in the mouth and resist working correctly by keeping the hindquarters disengaged, thereby not over-tracking or working from behind into the bridle. As a consequence, the rider cannot develop the gaits to show any engagement, self-carriage, or even changes of tempo within the paces. The rider will have limited ability to bend the horse correctly, thereby making it very difficult to teach the horse higher level movements, such as lateral movements.

Very often horses that consistently stay behind the contact are also difficult to ride in a forward, active tempo. This has a negative effect on the quality of the delivery of the rider's aids, consequently, the pairing becomes a picture of discord and antagonism.

An ex-racehorse who has just started his re-training will not have the balance or relative engagement to stay connected to the bridle and maintain the poll as the highest point for long periods. They may briefly come off the bit, either too low or too high, but quickly find the aids again and reconnect. With intelligent and sympathetic riding, this is ok, and to be expected; they usually quickly allow themselves to be adjusted up to the contact. The problem becomes difficult to resolve if the horse learns to 'sit' behind the contact from early on in their re-training, with little or no correction from the rider.

There are a number of ways in which you can work with your horse to correct the problem of him coming behind the contact.

Step 1 - Make the horse more reactive to the 'go' aids, namely the legs and seat

The rider may need to use a whip to 'tick' the horse's hips in the rhythm of the tempo the rider wants to reinforce the forward meaning. The horse should learn to be helped with the whip and not become frightened by it.

Step 2 - Try not to ride with strong rein aids

Initially, it is better to ignore the position of the head and concentrate on maintaining prompt forward responses. When the prompt forward responses develop and become reliable, then you can incorporate 'useful', not antagonistic, rein (restraining) aids.

Step 3 - When the forward and restraining aids can be used collaboratively, allow the horse to build confidence and trust working within them

When the confidence builds, the horse will be able to connect onto the ends of the reins and from this, will be in a better position to keep the poll up and allow the rider to ride forwards into the bridle, not the other way around.

Slowly, over time the correctness and quality of the frame will improve and become more reliable, which will inevitably enable you to have more control of the horse and progression of the training.

Problem #8 – Lateral walk

A lateral walk is one in which the natural sequence of footfalls is disrupted. There should be four evenly spaced steps, not two steps, a gap and then two more steps. Listen as you ride down the road – you should hear clip-clop-clip-clop, and not clip-clop (gap) clip-clop.

One of the other terms for this type of walk is a 'camel walk'. If you watch camels move you will see the two legs on one side of the body move almost simultaneously, followed by the same on the opposite side.

Physically, a lateral walk is caused by tension in the horse's back muscles. To move in the correct sequence, each of the long back muscles (longissimus dorsi) must alternately contract and relax. If they are held tensely, without the ability to relax, the correct neuro-muscular sequence cannot take place, causing the broken rhythm.

Tension may be general, especially in an excitable or anxious horse, or it may be caused by the rider using a too strong and restrictive rein contact, often in an effort to put the horse on the bit, or to collect the walk, or to control jogging.

This is an extremely difficult, and sadly sometimes impossible, problem to correct. The best answer is not to allow it to occur in the first place. However, if you do have this issue, things you can try which may either help or possibly correct it are:

Relaxation whilst working

Anything that helps your horse to relax – hacking, turnout, natural calming products etc. The goal is to release the tension in your horse's back muscles.

Water

If possible, do lots of walking in water – deep puddles, or on a water treadmill, or in the sea. The drag of the water against the legs makes it almost impossible for the horse to walk laterally, so you may be able to resurrect the correct neuro-muscular sequence in his body.

Pole work

Walk over ground poles placed close together so he has to lift his legs higher rather than stretch for length. Use heavy wooden poles that are hard to move or raised poles with secure supports.

Always have someone present when you do pole work – horses can trip over even at walk.

Choose the correct speed

Take care not to hurry the walk as this will make it worse – but also don't allow dawdling, which can have the same effect.

Lateral movements

The use of lateral movements can help, particularly shoulder-in. If you can gain sufficient relaxation combined with the sideways steps, once again you can re-instill the correct sequence. This is also a technique that may help in competition, as you can put the horse into mild shoulder fore almost anywhere in a dressage test without upsetting the judge!

Problem #9 – Uneven contact

Some ex-racers find it very difficult to understand the concept of working into an even contact. That makes it almost impossible to develop the light, elastic contact and self-carriage that dressage demands.

If the contact feels heavy on one side, you must proactively ease and relax your hand on that side, while taking up a slightly stronger supportive contact on the other rein.

Try this exercise to correct the problem:

- Ride a 20-meter circle in trot.
- On the open part of the circle, ride a transition to walk, and then leg-

yield away from your inside leg.
- When the horse connects to your outside rein, pick up the trot again, and soften the inside rein.

Your horse should become steadier in your outside rein, and you should be able to turn right and left with equal ease, changing the horse from one outside rein to the other without resistance.

Problem #10 - On the forehand

When a horse is said to be, 'on the forehand' it means that the overall impression to the onlooker is that the majority of the weight is being carried on the horse's shoulders and front half.

Racehorses are always on the forehand because they are faster when they move that way. He also balances with momentum. Think of riding a bike, the slower you go the harder it is for you to stay balanced and upright. The same is true for the racehorse. He balances by going faster and by using his head and neck. This is now unacceptable and dangerous in the small confines of a dressage arena, so it's your job to teach him how to balance by using his hindquarters.

Before you set about correcting this fault, it's important to understand that at first your ex-racer won't be physically muscular and strong enough to be able to take the weight back onto his hindquarters, and it takes systematic and correct training over time to correct this.

Getting your horse off the forehand

Transitions between the paces and within them can help to engage the horse's hind legs and transfer his balance to his hindquarters.

Working on transitions around a circle will also serve to bring his inside hind leg more underneath him.

Lateral exercises such as leg yielding and shoulder-in are useful in engaging the hind legs. These can be combined with transitions for maximum effect.

If your horse tends to lose his balance onto his forehand through the transitions, try riding a few steps of shoulder-in as you approach the transition. Remember to keep your leg on, so that the horse doesn't lose impulsion as he makes the transition. You actually need *more* impulsion for a downward transition than for an upward one, in order to keep the hind leg traveling forward and underneath the horse to balance him as he makes the 'gear change' down.

Once your horse has begun to develop better engagement and is lighter in the forehand, you'll need to work on maintaining this balance and frame throughout a whole dressage test. You can do this by using half-halts to re-balance your horse before every transition, change of direction, or lateral movement.

Problem #11 - Poor rhythm in walk and trot

Racehorses are used to working in a rhythm, but that's primarily in canter and gallop! When you ask your ex-racer to walk or trot, he may find it difficult to maintain a regular rhythm. Sometimes, the walk will become lateral, usually because the horse is tense. Jogging in the walk is also a common issue that can be very tiring for both parties.

Many ex-racers work in too quick a tempo. That's not surprising, bearing in mind that the horse has been taught to go fast, and the problem is exacerbated by the horse's lack of understanding of the basic seat, hand, and leg aids.

Watching your horse working on the lunge will help you to see whether the rhythm is correct. If everything is fine without the addition of a rider, but problems occur when the horse is ridden, look to yourself and your riding first. Remember that if you're tense and tight, anticipating fireworks, your horse will pick up the vibe immediately! If your horse thinks that you're worried about something, his natural flight instinct will kick in, and your horse will immediately switch to racing mode, ready to run away from the perceived danger. Take a deep breath and try to relax as much as possible. Let your seat sink deep into the saddle, follow the horse's movement, and allow with your hand so that the horse can work calmly forward.

Sometimes, problems with the rhythm occur because the horse is being pushed out of his comfort zone too early in his dressage career. Be sure to progress systematically and steadily up the levels, keeping the Scales of Training to the forefront of your mind. Pushing your horse for too much too soon usually results in a loss of balance or excessive tension that eventually corrupts the correct rhythm.

Problem #12 - Lacks straightness

Straightness is ultimately achieved by making sure that the scales of rhythm, suppleness, contact, and impulsion are in place.

The correct rhythm in all paces for a dressage horse is paramount and should be established first. In that **rhythm**, the horse should swing through a *supple* back into an elastic even **contact**, and with **active** hindquarters. Only when the rider can achieve all these elements of the scales, can they make the horse straight.

<u>Walk</u>

In walk, because the horse's hindquarters are wider than his shoulders and the walk moves slowly, the horse can wiggle and crab. Keep the walk moving forward and encourage the horse to work into the contact.

If the horse comes against the hand, this blocking action will cause the quarters to swing in, so make sure that the contact is light and remains elastic.

Keep the horse's neck straight; too much neck bend will cause the horse's shoulder to bulge out.

<u>Trot</u>

It can be easier to keep the horse straight in trot because it's easier to ride him forward.

First of all, make sure that you're sitting straight and that your weight is evenly distributed over your seat bones. You can't expect your horse to stay straight if you're sitting to one side! Keep both legs on equally and ride forward into an even rein contact down both reins. Check that your hands are carried at the same height with thumbs on top. Now, ride your horse forward.

<u>Canter</u>

Keeping your horse straight in canter can be tricky. Horses that are unbalanced in the canter often compensate by bringing their quarters to the inside to avoid taking more weight on their hind legs. You can compensate for this by riding a half-halt and bringing your horse's shoulders in very slightly from the track. This helps to keep the quarters out and stops the horse from becoming crooked.

Problem #13 - Opening mouth

Whatever the reason for your horse working with his mouth open, DO NOT resort to forcing the horse's mouth shut by using a tight flash or crank noseband, as that will only lead to more misery for the horse and create even greater resistance and evasion.

First of all, put the horse on the lunge in just a cavesson or headcollar. Does the horse trot around on the lunge with his mouth wide open? If he does, it's most likely that the evasion has become a habit or is a sign of another underlying issue. However, if the mouth stays shut, then the horse is only displaying discomfort whilst being ridden.

Such discomfort can be caused by:

- Dental problems
- The rider's unsteady hands (constantly pulling or seesawing at the horse's mouth)
- A poorly fitting bit
- Tension
- A combination of the above

Let's look at each individually.

Dental check

First of all, you should make sure that your hose is up to date with his dental examinations. Any sharp edges or hooks could be causing the horse discomfort when you pick up a contact with the bit.

Poorly fitting bit

If the horse's bit doesn't fit him properly, he may open his mouth to escape the discomfort it is causing.

For the horse to be comfortable in his mouth, he must be able to move his jaw freely, from side-to-side. When the horse has a bit in his mouth, he salivates, and so he needs to be able to swallow. When the horse swallows, his tongue is lifted toward his palate. If the bit is painful, too thick, is held too strongly by the rider's hand, or if the horse has his jaw clamped shut by a noseband, he will be unable to lift his tongue and swallow, and his jaw will remain tense. The horse will then push back against the bit with his tongue in an attempt to lift it so that he can swallow. That leads to tension not only in the horse's tongue but in his neck and jaw too.

The bit should not protrude from either side of the horse's mouth, and it should not be too thick or thin. If the bit is too small, it will pinch the horse's lips. If the bit sits too high or too low in the horse's mouth, it can crash against his teeth, causing him discomfort.

As well as fitting the bit correctly, you must choose one that suits your horse as every horse's mouth is unique in size and shape. To find the best bit for your horse, ask an experienced bit-fitting service for advice, and be prepared to experiment. Your horse will soon tell you what bit he prefers and how it should be fitted for his comfort.

Unsteady hands

If your unsteady hands are causing the problem, you'll need to work on developing a more independent seat. That will enable you to ride in a secure balance and with quiet hands.

Never use the reins for balance; your hands should always work independently of your seat.

So, how do you know if your hands are unsteady? Try dropping your little finger onto your horse's neck and see if you can keep it there while the horse is trotting and cantering. If you can't keep your pinkie in touch with the horse's neck, your hands are bouncing.

Once you've improved your seat and your unsteady hands are no longer the issue, you can start to work on undoing your horse's evasive habit.

Try lungeing your horse in side reins with elasticated inserts or "donut" rings. The consistent, elastic contact provided by the side reins helps to teach your horse that reaching for the bit isn't uncomfortable anymore. Working on a circle also encourages relaxation and helps to create a good rhythm.

Another helpful exercise that you can try is to work your horse over low cavaletti or poles on the ground. That encourages the horse to stretch forward and down. Once the horse understands that he can trust your hands to be quiet and soft, he will begin to reach for the bit.

Tension

Tension can cause a horse to develop the habit of working with his mouth open, even though there is no physical discomfort involved.

A horse that is tense may sometimes express his anxiety by showing resistance to the contact and opening his mouth. In this scenario, your goal is to encourage relaxation.

How you can solve the problem of tension depends on what the root cause is. It may be that desensitization will help to solve the problem, or perhaps working the horse in the company of an experienced older animal may be effective.

Problem #14 - Cantering on the incorrect leg

Canter transitions tend to happen in a rushed and unbalanced way, and often, ex-racers are accustomed to cantering more on one leading leg than the other, so they can initially find it difficult to adjust to cantering on both leads equally.

Here are two exercises that are extremely helpful in teaching your horse to canter on the correct leg.

Step 1

This first step is done in the walk and is a brilliant way of improving rider coordination.

Remember to ride the whole exercise in the walk. Don't move into canter yet; this exercise is designed to make sure that **you** understand how and when to use the canter aids.

To pick up left canter:

1. Drop your weight into your left seat bone.
2. Gently flex the horse to the left.
3. Keep a contact on your right rein (outside rein) to prevent the horse's neck from bending too much to the left. You should just be able to see the horse's inside eye, not the whole side of his face.
4. Your left leg is on the girth, asking the horse to pick up the canter.
5. Your right leg should be slightly behind the girth, asking the horse's right hind leg to strike off into left canter. (Note that the horse must begin the canter stride with his outside hind leg so that he finishes up on the correct lead.)
6. Keep this "left canter lead" position for a few walk steps and then change your aids as if you were asking for the right lead canter.

Step 2

This next step utilizes the aids you learned in the walk. But this time, you're going to ride the exercise in trot, and then ask the horse to canter.

1. Position the horse slightly to the inside, as you did in the walk

exercise above. Keep your outside rein secure to prevent the horse from drifting out through his shoulder.
2. When you ask the horse to canter, push forward with your inside seat bone toward the horse's inside ear.
3. Use a small squeeze with your inside leg on the girth to ask the horse to go forward into canter.
4. Use your outside leg a couple of inches behind the girth to tell the horse to strike-off into canter with his outside hind leg.

Assuming there are no physiological reasons, if you are still struggling to get the horse to strike off on the correct leg, then it's usually down to one (or a combination, of the following reasons.

Reason #1 – Not enough bend toward the leading leg

If your horse picks up the wrong lead, it's possible that you didn't keep the inside bend through the horse's body and the inside flexion at his poll during the transition. As a general rule, the horse will pick up whatever canter lead he is bent and flexed toward.

Correct the problem as follows, using either of these techniques:

1. Ride a small circle to establish the correct bend. Just before you end the circle, keep the bend, and then ask for the canter transition. As soon as the horse picks up canter on the correct lead, reward him by moving him out onto a larger circle.
2. Walk or trot around a small circle. Leg-yield out onto a larger circle before asking for canter. Use your inside leg on the girth during the leg-yield to help keep the bend. When riding a circle to the right, picture yourself pushing your horse's rib cage to the left, while keeping his neck and hindquarters to the right.

Reason #2 – Too much neck bend

A uniform bend throughout the horse's body will encourage him to step underneath himself with his inside hind leg, improving his balance, and making it easier for him to strike off on the correct leading leg. However, a common rider fault is to ask for too much neck bend, allowing the horse to fall out through the shoulder. When that happens, the horse will drift sideways when you ask him to canter and will probably either stay in trot or strike off on the incorrect leg, because of the misalignment of his body.

Reason #3 – Unbalanced, hurried trot

If the horse is allowed to become unbalanced and run onto his forehand in the trot, he will most likely trot faster and faster, rather than transitioning into canter. So, steady the trot tempo and use your half-halts to bring the horse's balance back onto his hindquarters before asking him to canter.

Reason #4 – Unbalanced rider

Sometimes, the rider unbalances the horse by tipping forward as they ask for canter. The horse responds by falling randomly into canter to save himself and his rider from stumbling, often resulting in an incorrect strike-off. So, as you apply the canter aids, sit up straight and look forward, not down at the ground.

Problem #15 - Tight and hollow through the topline

Racehorses are not required to work through their topline in the same way that dressage horses are, and often, the ex-racer has a large muscle underneath their neck, just where you don't want it!

Over time, systematic and correct schooling will help the horse to build muscle in the right areas. He will then become strong enough to cope with the demands made by his new career, and his natural downhill way of going will slowly become more uphill.

To achieve that, you will first need to teach your horse to work in a round outline. A correct acceptance of the bit is integral to this. The horse must be able to softly chew the bit, which is integral to flexibility at the poll.

Provided the above components are in place, improving the suppleness over the back is then a matter of frequent variations of the outline, putting the horse up into a shorter, taller frame for a short period, followed by stretching down and round.

Within the stretched frame, you can do exercises such as leg yield and smaller circles to further elasticize the top line.

Trotting over poles with a lower round frame is also valuable, but you should always ensure that someone is with you in case your horse trips over!

Lungeing in low-positioned side reins, trotting up hills with a lower neck frame, and riding in jump (or light) seat can all be valuable too.

Problem #16 - Lack of balance

Thoroughbreds are generally built on their forehand. While that's not a problem for a racehorse, it is for a dressage horse!

Unfortunately, when a horse is on his forehand, the downward transitions are usually rough and unbalanced, and cantering can feel as though you are falling off a cliff! To correct balance issues, you must first teach your ex-racer to work through his topline (as discussed above). That will allow you to ride effective half-halts, which will improve the horse's balance and ultimately help him to develop a more uphill way of going.

Transitions between the paces and within them can help to engage the horse's hind legs and transfer his balance to his hindquarters. Working on transitions around a circle will also serve to bring the horse's inside hind leg more underneath him.

Lateral exercises such as leg yielding and shoulder-in are useful in engaging the hind legs. These can be combined with transitions for maximum effect.

If your horse tends to lose his balance onto his forehand through the transitions, try riding a few steps of shoulder-in as you approach the transition. Remember to keep your leg on, so that the horse doesn't lose impulsion as he makes the transition.

Problem #17 - Lateral stiffness

Your ex-racer will be stiff laterally. That is, he won't show a uniform bend around circles, and he will most likely be crooked on straight lines too.

When you're riding circles, the horse may fall out or fall in. Instead of engaging his inside hind leg to carry his weight and that of his rider through the movement, the horse either stiffens against your inside leg and leans inwards or ignores your outside aids and drifts out through his outside shoulder.

<u>Falling in</u>

The only way to train your horse not to fall in around circles and corners is by consistently riding him from your inside leg to your outside hand. Insist that your horse stays upright and doesn't lean on your leg as a prop.

If necessary, give your horse a sharp kick or a flick with your schooling whip just behind your inside leg to remind him that it's there to be respected and is not being provided specially for him to lean on!

Similarly, the horse should not be allowed to lean on your outside rein. Give and take the rein every few steps to make sure that the horse is not allowing you to carry him around the outside of the circle.

<u>Falling out</u>

To prevent the horse from falling out, you'll need to straighten his neck by using your outside rein. To do that, shut your outside elbow tighter against your body, and don't pull backward on the rein.

At the same time, step into your inside stirrup, and shift your weight onto your inside seat bone. Don't lean to the left; straighten the side of your body so that it becomes longer from your armpit.

Turn your upper body to the inside so that your outside shoulder and hand travel forward, and your inside shoulder and hand move back. That brings your outside hand forward and inward towards the horse's crest, allowing the bend but still containing the horse's outside shoulder.

Bring your inside hand away from the neck, as if you are leading the horse around the circle or through a turn. Turn from your waist, not your hips.

If you find that the horse is drifting off a straight line, keep the hand on that side closed against the horse's shoulder, and ride more positively forward to help straighten him.

Problem #18 - Hacking out – napping

Most racehorses are accustomed to hacking out in a string, either on their way to the gallops or for exercise. So, your horse may be used to seeing traffic, road markings, etc. However, although hacking out in company is probably not going to be a problem, flying solo can be a different matter.

Horses that nap generally lack confidence and trust in their rider. Horses are herd animals, and they look to the guidance of a leader. That leadership begins on the ground in your everyday relationship with your horse and in groundwork, such as long-reining and lungeing.

Napping usually happens when you try to take the horse out on his own without the companionship of an equine "nanny." The horse often simply stops and refuses to move forward. Some horses even refuse to turn around and go back toward home! They became so frightened of the world that standing still frozen to the spot is their preferred action.

So, if your horse starts napping, keep his feet moving, regardless of whether that's forward or sideways. The horse will quickly learn that it's easier to go forward!

When you put your leg on, your horse must react. Don't nag with your leg and allow the horse to hesitate before he responds. You'll need to be consistent and insist on that response both in the schooling arena and when you're out hacking.

Don't give up! If you're struggling, always seek professional help, ideally from someone who is experienced in handling and re-training ex-racers.

Other problems?

If you are having any other training problems, pop boy our website HowToDressage.com and check out our 'Troubleshooting' category where you will find lots of articles.

If you cannot find the answer to your problem, then please feel free to email us at hello@howtodressage.com and we can either point you in the right direction or get one of our dressage judges to write a new article with the solution.

SCHOOLING STRUCTURE

Whatever your competitive level and aspirations, a structured training plan for your horse is a crucial tool that allows you to advance in the dressage arena.

Keep it varied

One of the most common setbacks experienced by dressage riders is that their horses become stale and bored because of over-training. Sometimes, an over-schooled horse will become resistant or disobedient, possibly because he is physically sore or simply because he is fed up with doing the same thing.

In general, most horses will do well with three or four days of dressage training per week. You should include other activities such as hacking, jumping, and lungeing and your horse will appreciate a rest day turned out in the field!

Your schooling routine structure

Every schooling session should include a warm-up, a training phase, and a cool-down phase.

Let's look at each of those phases individually.

1. The warm-up phase

The idea of the warm-up phase is to allow your horse to stretch his muscles and loosen his body in preparation for the training section of his workout.

Begin with an energetic walk on a long rein and some basic preliminary or training level work, including large circles, transitions in and out of the working paces, and some center lines.

All your trot work should be done rising so that the horse can use his back freely. Your aim here is to warm up the horse's muscles, get his cardiovascular system working, and loosen his joints so that he can work without risk of injury.

The way in which you ride your horse may contradict his nature. For example, if the horse is inclined to be lazy, you might need to kick-on and really wake him up. On the other hand, if your horse tends to be "hot" and stressy, you might need to use a slower, more relaxed chill-out routine. The warm-up is definitely a case of "horses for courses."

Gradually, the warm-up will include your horse's confirmed level of work, enabling you to find out what he finds easy and what he sees as a greater challenge, both physically and attitudinally. So, the greater your horse's repertoire, the more time it will take to warm him up.

The warm-up is a good way of evaluating and identifying where your horse is at in his training and allows you to determine the focus of the training phase of your schooling plan. Also, the warm-up allows you to know how long it takes for your horse to be "in the zone" and ready to perform a test. So, when you go to a competition, you will know exactly how long your working-in period should be.

2. The training phase

Once your horse is warm and mentally focused on the aids, you can begin the training phase of your schooling session.

Ideally, your horse should be working forward from behind through his back and into an elastic contact. However, in practice, and depending on the level at which your horse is working, you may need to begin the training phase of your schooling session when you get an acceptable reaction to your basic aids.

The training phase of every schooling session should be based around how the horse does things, not on what he can do. In other words, you must always work to ensure that the basics are in place before moving on to teaching your horse "tricks," such as half-pass, flying changes, etc.

So, the training phase must always be based around The Training Scales (see page 116). The training scale tells you how to challenge your horse, and it also reminds you when you've pushed him too far. When riding on your own, the training scale helps to identify the prerequisites to working up through the levels, which, in turn, teaches you to "listen" to your horse. For example, if the rhythm starts to suffer or there's resistance to the contact, you know you are asking too much of the horse, and you should take a step back. Find out what's caused the problem: perhaps take a walk break, lighten your hand or seat, or try giving your horse a sympathetic pat, and then begin work again.

When you move into the training phase of your schooling session, concentrate on developing more impulsion, which is crucial for prelim or first level horses. Riding transitions within the paces helps to engage the horse's joints and release the energy that you need for true impulsion. Novice level tests ask you to show a few steps of medium trot, which is a good indicator of whether the horse is working forward with impulsion or not.

In elementary or second level work, straightness is crucial, as that enables collection. The lateral exercises that you ride at this level provide you with the tools that you need to build the horse's strength, symmetry, and straightness. So, when you move on to work on the next level of your horse's training, you will be able to ride him in collection for brief periods.

Now, technically, the foundation of your work is complete. However, your training from now right through Grand Prix will focus on improving each element of the training scales; rhythm, throughness, contact, impulsion, and collection, as well as developing self-carriage and relaxation. Here are some extra tips to help you achieve that.

Tip #1 – A little bit of stress promotes growth

When schooling your horse, challenge him with work that stresses him *just a little*. Horses learn best when challenged with new work, so essentially, no stress means no improvement or progress.

You must assess what level, type, and duration of stress works for your horse. Horses that get tense and stressy do best with a routine to their schooling program. When presented with a new challenge, these horses respond by getting upset. Then it's up to you to reassure the horse and return to their familiar, comfortable routine. If you introduce stress in very small increments, your horse will happily learn to accept that, because he learns that each of those small doses of stress becomes part of his routine and are always followed by resolution and relief.

At the opposite end of the scale are horses that are easily bored. These horses thrive when presented with a new challenge and relish a change in routine that prevents them from becoming stale.

Although the Scale of Training shows you how to challenge your horse, it also serves as a reminder of when you've pushed too far. If the base of the training pyramid begins to crumble, you know that the stress levels you've placed on your horse are a step too far, and you need to take a step back into the horse's comfort zone. For example, if the horse starts to lose rhythm because you've pushed him too much in an attempt to build impulsion, that should warn you to adopt a less aggressive approach to your training. So, before presenting your horse with a new challenge, make sure that the basic foundations are in place.

If your horse becomes upset or unsettled when presented with a new challenge, you'll need to work out how to recover the lost quality. A gentle pat, a few kind words, lightening your aids, a walk break, or maybe even a short burst to release pent up energy and frustration; all of these tactics can be effective, but once again, it's really a matter of horses for courses. What works for one horse may not work for another.

When it comes to deciding how long to labor a particular point, the best tactic is to train for long enough that the horse recognizes and partially meets the new challenge. However, don't keep pushing on so that the horse can't recover his equilibrium quickly. Provided that the horse learns that he can attempt to meet the challenge with which he's presented, and he will quickly be rewarded for his efforts, all should proceed positively, and the horse won't fear the stress.

When a new training concept is still unclear to the horse, repetition can help to train a certain degree of anticipation that can work for you. You must be careful not to punish the horse for anticipating your instructions, although he must learn to wait for you and not execute the movement before you ask him to.

For example, if you are working on simple changes, don't reprimand the horse for anticipating the downward transition if that means he's beginning to "sit" and bring his hocks underneath his body. That's a good thing, as it means the downward transition will be nicely balanced, and the upward transition will be uphill and fluent.

Tip #2 – Training the walk

The inclusion of frequent walk breaks in the training phase is a beneficial tactic.

Firstly, the horse learns that walking doesn't mean that work is over for the day! That's important when it comes to riding a dressage test; you don't want your horse to think he's finished as soon as you get to the walk exercises!

Walking also allows the horse to get his breath back between bouts of more strenuous work, gradually increasing his stamina and strength, and allows tired muscles and joints to recover.

Working your horse in the walk while keeping him on the aids is a skill in itself. Walk breaks on a long or loose rein present you with an opportunity to evaluate what you've achieved to date, plan the next phase of training, and rest the horse's body between efforts. However, by keeping your horse on the aids during his walk breaks, you're ensuring that he is physically and mentally prepared to continue with good quality work when you ask him to.

If that habit is not well-established, you'll find that the horse has gone "off the boil" during the walk from the working-in area to the arena. However, if you get into the habit of restarting several times during each training session, the horse will happily return to work mode in both the schooling and competition arena.

Tip #3 – Using the dressage tests in your training plan

The dressage tests are all numbered sequentially, beginning with the simplest. In theory, the higher the number, the more challenging the work contained in the test will be. So, a useful exercise you can do from your armchair on a cold, wet day is to spend time looking through each test and making a note of the different movements it contains. You can then use your list as a basis for your training plan. So, once your horse can perform everything at Prelim and Novice level to a good standard, you know he's ready to move on to Elementary, etc.

Using the dressage tests as a basis for your training plan also allows you to vary the exercises you use during the training phase so that the work doesn't become repetitive and boring for your horse.

Tip #4 – Blending exercises

Using random exercises can be beneficial to your horse's training, but you will often achieve better results if you blend different exercises into short routines as part of your daily training.

For example, riding shoulder-in around a circle helps to bring the horse's hind legs closer together, which in turn makes it easier to collect, straighten, and balance the horse on a straight line.

So, by blending a mixture of bent and straight lines in shoulder-in, you will improve the horse's balance, suppleness, and engagement. Ultimately, the horse will find performing the shoulder-in on a straight line just as easy as he does on a circle, and his overall way of going will also improve as a result.

Tip #5 – Learning should be fun!

Too much repetition can be tedious for both the horse and the rider. So, change things around and think outside the box!

Learning can and should be fun! So, adopt a more playful attitude to your work.

Why not leg-yield from one side of the trail to the other while out hacking?

Or perhaps, ride travers between two poles on the ground, and then canter to the end of the arena. When you ride with a playful attitude, there are no rules. Have fun, and you'll be amazed at what you can achieve.

"Playing" with your horse helps to strengthen him physically, teaches him new skills, and keeps him fresh. You may even find that the standard exercises in dressage tests seem simple in comparison to what you have achieved when the two of you are just playing!

Here's an example of how you can use playing to train a novice horse to easily accomplish an elementary level exercise, as well as introducing him to more advanced skills:

Simple changes, tempis, and canter pirouettes!

Start by thinking of the simple changes as an auditory rhythm exercise. So, listen to the sound of canter-walk-canter:

Da-da-dum, da-da-dum, da-da-dum, da-da-BUM-BUM-BUM (walk), da-da-dum, da-da-dum, da-da-dum, da-da-BUM-BUM-BUM (walk)

Now, with that rhythm in your mind, ride the simple changes as if they were temp changes across the diagonal. So, canter four strides, walk three strides, canter four strides on the opposite leg, and so forth.

Make the exercise more challenging by riding simple changes down the centerline every four strides. Then try the same exercise, making a simple change every three strides. That's a fabulous exercise to engage, straighten, and sensitize a horse while also confirming the simple changes.

Keep playing with this routine until the elementary level exercise of one single simple change over X seems ridiculously easy in comparison.

When you train simple changes this well, you are laying the groundwork for canter pirouettes. A perfect simple change requires the horse to load his hind leg as he would do in a canter pirouette. Turning the pirouette is relatively easy.

So, when the simple change feels easy, introduce a quarter canter pirouette instead of the walk transition element of the change. That allows you to play with pirouettes long before you need to ride them "for real." The horse will understand that pirouettes are simply an extension of what he can already do well.

Tip #6 – Gifts from your horse!

In dressage training, one thing very often follows another as you move along the training scale. However, your horse will give you unexpected gifts from time-to-time that you must recognize and use to your advantage.

For example, your horse might make a flying change when you're riding in a counter-canter. Rather than regarding such events as evasions and reprimanding your horse, you should appreciate the unexpected gift. You can then sort out the misunderstanding. The important thing is to recognize the horse for the effort he's made.

Tip #7 – Learning to listen

Try to listen for the feel of the advanced horse within your inexperienced novice or elementary level mount. The only way that your horse will know that he's doing the right thing is if you let him know!

Just as learning to work along the scales of training is a skill that your horse must learn, listening to your horse is a skill that you need to learn.

Here are some tips that will help you to learn to listen to your horse so that you can ultimately work together in perfect harmony:

- Develop the ability to follow your horse's movement underneath you. The best way to do that is to have some lunge lessons.
- Develop a balanced, independent seat that enables you to hold your position, regardless of what your horse is doing underneath you. Again, the best way to achieve that is on the lunge.
- Next, develop influence so that you can be proactive and stabilize your position simultaneously.
- Learn to listen to your horse underneath you so that you can "hear" when your horse is losing his balance or drifting away from you.
- Now deliberately ride out of harmony with your horse and ask him to come to you.
- When the horse joins you, you will achieve the ultimate, elusive harmony that makes the difference between a good dressage test and an exceptional one.

The point of the exercise is that your horse enjoys that feeling of being in perfect harmony with you as much as you do. So, when the feeling isn't harmonious, the horse tries to find the feeling. Riders who ride their horses in this way can achieve something special without having to continually "tell" their horses; the horses come to them.

3. The cool-down phase

All professional athletes include a cool-down phase, both in their training sessions and in competition. And your horse is no different!

Cooling down helps to prevent injury and muscle stiffness, and it's crucial to your horse's wellbeing.

When you've finished the training phase of your workout, finish off each schooling session with a few simple exercises in rising trot that allow the horse to stretch his muscles and loosen his back, followed by a period of walking on a long rein.

By allowing your horse to cool down in this way, you are showing him that periods of hard work are always followed by things that he can do easily. The winding down work teaches the horse that he can finish his schooling session feeling that the work is easy, and he feels great.

The duration of the cool-down will depend on the intensity and difficulty of the training phase. So, you may need to cool down your horse for between 10 and 20 minutes. This period of relaxation is just as important to the horse's wellbeing as the warm-up.

The cooling-off walk allows the horse's heart to slow down, lets his circulation return to normal, and prevents the horse's muscles from stiffening-up when he is at rest. Also, the horse's footfalls help to pump blood out of the extremities before he is returned to his stable. If you don't allow sufficient time for that, soundness and circulatory problems can occur.

Keep a training diary

To help keep track of our horse's training routine, we highly advise you keep a diary. Not only is this a fantastic thing to be able to look back on to see how far you have both progressed, it will help to keep you focused on your training goals and schedule your horse's work accordingly.

You can use a simple notepad, or you can grab a copy of our "Ultimate Dressage Training Diary" specifically designed for this purpose. You can find out more information about our diaries on our Facebook Page or on Amazon.

SECTION FIVE:
HOW TO START COMPETING YOUR EX-RACEHORSE IN DRESSAGE

ABOUT DRESSAGE TESTS

Before you begin competing your ex-racehorse in dressage, it's a good idea to first understand the purpose of a dressage test and what the judges will be looking for at each level.

What's the purpose of dressage tests?

Every dressage test is designed to allow the dressage judge to assess the horse's competence at that level. If the training has been skimped on and the basic foundations are not in place, each test will expose any shortcomings!

The tests are designed to be tackled in order. The lower the number of the test, the easier it is. Each test contains exercises that are specifically formulated to assess how the horse's basic training is progressing.

Training/Preliminary level tests

The purpose of training/preliminary level tests is to show that the horse is developing the first three aspects of the Scales of Training:

- The horse should work in the correct rhythm and steady tempo at each pace.
- The horse's back should be loose and supple, without tension.
- The contact should be elastic and consistent, and the outline should be correct and steady.

First/Novice level tests

The first/novice level tests are designed to show that the horse can now demonstrate the correct basics required at training/preliminary level.

By now, the horse should also be able to show that he is beginning to develop impulsion so that he works forward from behind, through a supple back, into a steady, elastic contact.

Second, third, fourth/elementary/medium level tests

Once the horse reaches elementary level, the first four Scales of Training should be in place. The horse should demonstrate a greater level of straightness, suppleness to the bend, balance, self-carriage, and throughness than was present in the earlier levels.

Elementary and medium level tests ask for more well-defined and engaged transitions between the paces. The straightness, suppleness to the bend, self-carriage, throughness, and balance should now be well-established.

What are dressage judges looking for?

When it comes to competition, dressage judges are looking for a horse that works correctly along the Scales of Training (more on page 116).

In summary, the judge will be marking you and your horse on the following basic criteria:

- The rhythm in each pace must be correct and regular
- The horse should be relaxed and free from tension, working in harmony with his rider.
- The horse should work freely forwards from behind through a loose, swinging back.
- The horse should willingly accept an elastic rein contact. His mouth should remain closed, and he should not tilt his head or come "above the bit."
- The horse should work forwards with plenty of power generated by his hindquarters.

- The horse should move on one track, including around circles and through corners.
- The horse should be able to maintain his balance through transitions and around turns.
- Ideally, the horse should move "uphill" supported by and propelled by his hindquarters, rather than pulling himself along on his forehand.
- Lateral work should be correctly and consistently positioned, with fluent, light, supple steps.

As you and your horse move up through the levels of dressage competition, the judge will look for a higher degree of balance, collection, and suppleness, but the basic requirements remain the same.

EX-RACER ONLY COMPETITONS

Retrained racehorses are eligible for special events and championships where you will be competing only against other ex-racers in different events, including dressage, showjumping, eventing, and showing.

The great thing about these competitions is that you won't find yourself up against horses that have been specially bred for the disciplines. For example, there will be no huge-moving warmbloods powering down the centerline in a retrained racehorse dressage championship! So, everyone competes on a level playing field.

What's on where I live?

Thanks to their growing popularity, most countries around the world have special events for ex-racers, all with similar eligibility criteria.

Here are some examples of organizations around the world which offer such events.

<u>United Kingdom</u>

In the UK, there's the Retraining of Racehorses (RoR) competition series that covers many disciplines, including:

- Dressage
- Showing
- Team chasing
- Endurance
- Showjumping
- Eventing

- Hunting
- Trailblazers
- Polo
- Polocrosse
- Horseball
- TREC

RoR runs over 120 events and 300 classes every year right across the country. They also hold residential camps and training clinics.

To be eligible to compete and attend any of these events, you must:

- be aged over 15 on 1 January of the year in which you wish to compete
- be a member of RoR (membership is free) and hold a Competition Membership
- horses must be registered with RoR
- horses must have raced in Great Britain

More information can be found at www.ror.org.uk

United States

In the US, the Thoroughbred Incentive Program (TIP) run shows and awards in many disciplines, including:

- Eventing/combined training
- Dressage
- English pleasure
- Hunter classes
- Jumping
- Western
- Showing

- Polo
- Endurance

To be eligible for TIP classes and awards, the horse must have been registered with The Jockey Club or an equivalent Thoroughbred studbook that is approved by The Jockey Club and the International Stud Book Committee.

When attending shows, you'll need to prove your eligibility either by pre-entry or on the day of the show by presenting your TIP Number Card.

More information can be found at www.tjctip.com

New Zealand

In New Zealand, Beyond the Barriers (BtB) is an organization that promotes ex-racers as potential pleasure and sport horses. BtB runs various events, including a series specifically aimed at horses who have had less than 12 months' re-training.

As far as eligibility is concerned, horses are confined to three stages of classifications, depending on how long they have been in re-training. These divisions are designed to ensure a fair and appropriate level of opportunities for thoroughbreds across the board.

More information can be found at www.beyondthebarriers.co.nz

Australia

Any horse that was bred for racing, whether or not it actually ran under rules, is eligible for membership of Off The Track Western Australia. OTTWA organizes lots of events in a wide range of disciplines and training courses specifically for ex-racers.

To be eligible, you'll need to provide your horse's race name, microchip, or brands when you enter classes.

More information can be found at www.offthetrackwa.com.au

What now?

Ex-racehorse organizations can be great starting pointing, regardless of if you want to compete or not. Many of them offer training events, clinics, and free training advice to help you make the most of your OTTB and to help you progress.

We have detailed only one organization for each of the main areas, but with a bit of Googling you'll find many more that you will be able to get involved with.

COMPETING AGAINST OTHER BREEDS

Your ex-racehorse is eligible for some competitions that are specifically aimed at the breed. In fact, your horse may even have to have raced or been in training to qualify for such events. (Please see previous chapter)

However, most classes at regular dressage shows are open to all shapes and sizes of horses, including your ex-racer. So, what chance does your former racehorse have against those big-moving warmbloods?

Do horses with the best paces always win?

In a word, "No!" Dressage judges are required to judge **every** horse that comes down the centerline on the same scale, regardless of whether the horse is a $50,000 warmblood, a tiny pony, or a retired racehorse. All dressage judges should assess every horse to the same standard judging criteria, regardless of the horse's breed, movement, and type.

Dressage is a French word that literally means "training." So, ultimately, it should be the horse that is most correctly trained that is awarded the highest score. If a horse with big paces is not trained correctly, he won't get a high mark for the overall work, although the paces mark would probably still be a good one.

However, if an ex-racehorse with correct but "plain" paces demonstrates good rhythm, regularity, suppleness through his back, acceptance of an elastic contact, a lively impulsion, straightness, and good balance, he will always be awarded a higher mark than the flashy mover who shows none of those qualities.

Also, the regularity of the paces is absolutely crucial in dressage. The flashy-moving horse with an irregular trot or an incorrect walk will always finish up down at the bottom of the line, regardless of how well-schooled he is. Period.

Another particularly important point to note when discussing big-moving horses versus thoroughbreds is that warmbloods are not always the easiest beasts to ride! That massive, bouncy trot can be a nightmare to sit to, and the huge length of stride can be almost impossible to balance in canter.

What advantages do ex-racers have?

When it comes to dressage, your ex-racer has several advantages over many other breeds.

First of all, thoroughbreds are usually extremely intelligent and quick to learn. They soak up new lessons like sponges, which is a great advantage when you consider that you are teaching your horse from scratch.

Also, dressage demands that the horse works with enthusiasm and energy to make the most of his natural paces. Most thoroughbreds are pretty forward going, once they understand your leg, seat, and rein aids.

As for paces, it's said that if a horse has a good walk, it can also gallop, which is critical for a racehorse! So, most thoroughbreds do have an exceptionally good walk, and that's essential for a dressage horse.

What disadvantages do ex-racers have?

Unfortunately, ex-racers do have a few quirks that can be problematic for a dressage career, but no breed/type is perfect, and these issues can be trained and improved upon.

Firstly, the thoroughbred's conformation tends to be rather downhill and during his racing career he is taught to put most of his weight on his forehand. Dressage demands the exact opposite! The horse should take more weight on his hindquarters and move in an uphill cadence and balance. Although you cannot change your horse's conformation, you can train him to take less weight on his forehand and to carry more weight behind. For help with this, check out page 163.

Tension can be another bugbear in thoroughbred horses, especially when they're ridden in an unfamiliar environment, and that can also adversely affect the paces. Relaxation and harmony are crucial for good dressage, and a tense, tight horse will never be awarded high marks, regardless of his breeding. That said, relaxation is something that you can work on and improve over time, check out page 149 for more help with this.

Finally, at first, ex-racers can find cantering in an arena and negotiating small circles incredibly difficult! But again, that's an element of your horse's schooling work that you can gradually improve upon as your horse becomes more balanced and takes more weight behind.

Where can you pick up marks?

Despite the challenges that ex-racers face when compared to more traditionally bred dressage horses, there's no reason why you can't get good dressage scores, provided that your ex-racer is trained correctly according to The Scales of Training. (See page 116)

Also, every dressage test contains movements where you can pick up valuable marks. For example, walk pirouettes, rein-back, and the halt can all be performed well by any type/breed of horse, including an ex-racer.

Other places where you can earn good marks, regardless of how your horse moves are:

- Straight, accurate centerlines
- Correctly positioned, fluent lateral work
- Accurate circles
- Well-balanced transitions
- Good use of the arena, including riding into the corners and right up to the boards

Above all, make sure that you understand the geometry of the arena and ride every movement accurately.

Rider position and effect of the aids

Your own position and how you ride your horse will be marked in the collective section at the bottom of the test sheet. Obviously, if your horse goes well and you help rather than hinder him, you'll be awarded a good mark for the effect of your riding. A happy and harmonious partnership will also be marked highly.

So, by sitting correctly and riding your ex-racer effectively and sympathetically to good effect, you'll pick up extra marks in the rider and submission collectives.

Presentation

Regardless of the type of horse you have, good presentation can give a professional, pleasing impression to the judge.

A well-groomed, neatly plaited horse and smartly turned-out rider always make the judge feel that you've made an effort, and whilst there are no marks for turnout, image is important!

FIRST COMPETITIONS

So, after all those hours that you've invested in acclimating your ex-racer to his new home and taking his first tentative steps as a dressage horse in your home arena, your very first dressage competition is in sight!

Every horse is different. Some are naturally very laidback and don't find going to unfamiliar places exciting at all, whereas others just love going to "parties" and can barely contain their excitement. You must manage every situation according to your horse's reaction, and that's going to be a trial and error process at first until you get to know your horse.

Ultimately, your aim is to make the whole competition experience as enjoyable and stress-free as possible for you and for your horse. So, for your first few competitions together try not to focus too much on your score. Instead, focus on giving your horse positive experiences which you can then build upon.

All dressed up

Many former racehorses may be used to the idea of being plaited up and wearing traveling boots. However, simply being plaited can trigger anticipation and excitement in many ex-racers, as they have learned to associate that process with going to the races.

Try plaiting the horse up, and then working him in your home arena. Put him back in his box, leave him to relax for an hour or so, and then work him again. That helps the horse to understand that plaiting and grooming doesn't necessarily mean racing. It simply means work. It's also a good tactic to put your horse's full travel gear, including boots or bandages, a travel rug, headguard, etc. Watch the horse for his reaction to that. Some horses show truly little interest, whereas others are immediately on their toes.

Practice journeys

The key to success, as well as diligently and patiently schooling your horse, is preparing him for an unfamiliar and potentially exciting experience.

Remember that your horse's last couple of journeys were probably to the rehabilitation center and then to his new home with you. So, don't be surprised if your ex-racer is a little uncertain about his next lorry ride.

Although ex-racers are generally familiar with traveling to events, your horse may be expecting to race when he arrives, especially when he can see, hear, and smell other horses around him when you arrive. So, your first job is to overwrite that expectation.

Start by getting your horse accustomed to traveling to different places and working. Hiring out a local arena which you can box your horse to is a good idea. You will be able to see how your horse handles the whole experience without the added pressure of having to compete.

Although most ex-racers will be confident and frequent travelers, some horses are not good travelers unless they have a companion to keep them company, and your ex-racer may have never travelled alone. So, if necessary, you'll may need to recruit a calm, sensible horse or pony to act as a traveling buddy for your ex-racers first few journeys.

Choose your first show venue carefully

When you're ready to compete for the first time, choose the test and venue wisely. The most sensible tactic is to select a quiet, local venue and enter a low-key competition.

There are several reasons for that.

Firstly, a short journey is less stressful for the horse and for you. The horse will by now, be accustomed to taking short rides in your lorry or trailer and working when he arrives at the destination. So, by taking him to a local show, you're replicating a situation to which he's already accustomed.

Secondly, a local riding club or unaffiliated competition will be quieter and less busy than a large affiliated event, so there's less going on that's likely to stress your horse. Do some research before you enter the event. Find out if on-site stabling is available for the day so that your horse doesn't have to stand in the lorry. Most racehorses are used to arriving at the racecourse and then spending a few hours in a stable before being prepared for their race. If the horse has to stand in your lorry for hours, he may become upset and agitated, so if you can stable him at the venue, all the better.

Thirdly, if your horse is inclined to be "hot," lungeing him before you get on board can be helpful. But not all venues allow lungeing, so check with the organizer before you enter. Also, hot horses are often easier to keep on top of (literally!) when ridden in the confines of an indoor arena, rather than outside. If this is the case, choose an event with a small indoor school.

Fourthly, competitions held on grass are to be avoided in the early days of your ex-racer's dressage career. It's difficult for an unbalanced or inexperienced horse to cope with slippery grass and potentially skimpy dressage boards, and you're also exposed on all sides if the event is in a large field. You don't want to find yourself in a windy carpark, struggling to fit studs in an excited racehorse's shoes, and the last thing you want on the day of your first show is to find yourself disappearing down the field in a blaze of glory if things get out of control!

What test to choose

When it comes to picking a dressage test for your ex-racehorse's very first competition, always choose one that's at least one level below that at which you're working at home.

The key to success is that both you and your horse feel super-confident and relaxed. So, pick a test that you both find easy, rather than pushing yourself and struggling.

Ride through the test a couple of times at home and practice any movements that are potentially likely to be challenging when ridden away from home under test conditions. If you're concerned that you might forget the test, recruit someone to go with you who can call the test for you or ask the event organizer for help. Many venues have helpers available to call tests for competitors, in exchange for a small donation to a nominated charity.

Going it alone?

Most racing yards have a traveling head lad or lass who drives the lorry and takes care of checking-in at the racecourse, as well as supervising the horses. There's also usually a second pair of hands, and that's what you will need the first time that you take your ex-racer to a dressage show.

Bear in mind that your horse will be nervous and unsure of what's going on when you arrive at the venue, and you will have lots of things to think about and to get organized. Therefore, a knowledgeable helper will be invaluable to you on the day.

In the warm-up arena

Entering and exiting the warm-up arena is often the most challenging part of the day. Although your horse will be used to having other horses around him, he might get spooked if another rider passes too close to him or canters upsides while passing you. For that reason, it may be a good idea to put a red ribbon in your horse's tail. A red ribbon actually signifies a warning to other riders that your horse may kick if they get too close to him. But, even if that's not entirely true, a red ribbon will act as a useful deterrent to those who might otherwise crowd you.

Allow extra time for working-in. There will be lots of distractions, possibly including a tannoy system, spectators, food stalls, barking dogs, etc. Give your horse plenty to time to take everything in before you ask him to concentrate and settle down to his work. Use lots of transitions and changes of direction to keep your horse's mind on the job, and don't allow yourself to be distracted by what others are doing around you.

Often, problems start in earnest when it's time to leave the other horses in the working-in area and make your way to the test arena. That's where a helper comes in very handy. If necessary, you can ask your assistant to walk with you to the arena and stand close by where your horse can see them. That can be extremely reassuring for an ex-racer that's accustomed to being led around a parade ring and escorted to and from the racetrack.

Above all ...

The most important piece of advice for anyone taking an ex-racer to his first dressage competition is to **keep calm!**

No matter what happens, keep yourself relaxed and calm, and don't panic if things don't go quite according to plan. Remember that horses take their lead from their rider and handler. So, if you're able to remain relaxed and chilled-out, there's a good chance that your horse will do too.

Ultimately, it doesn't matter where you finish in the order on the results board. As long as you and your horse had an enjoyable, relaxed day out, then that's your mission accomplished, and a positive experience for your ex-racer is something that you can build upon.

Having too many expectations and putting too much pressure on yourself and your horse on your first competitive outing together is a recipe for disaster. So, take the pressure off and just enjoy the day together.

20 TIPS TO IMPROVE YOUR DRESSAGE SCORES

Dressage training is more of a marathon than a sprint, and you can't drastically improve your horse's way of going overnight. But there are some simple tactics you can employ immediately to improve your dressage test scores.

Here are our **20** top tips that you can use to gain you those valuable extra marks the next time you compete:

Before your go

There's a lot you can do to improve your dressage scores before you even put your horse on the lorry and drive to the event.

Here are a few simple ways to boost your percentage without even sitting on your horse!

Tip #1. Choose a dressage test that suits your horse

When choosing what tests to enter, listen to your horse!

All too often, riders enter a test that is either beyond their horse's current ability in the hope that it'll be okay on the day. So, pick a test that contains exercises that your horse can perform well and with confidence.

For example, if you have just begun competing in elementary level tests, make your competition debut with the most straightforward test of that level that your horse will find easy.

Tip #2. Don't upgrade too soon

Never try to run before you can walk!

It's much better to continue competing at the lower levels successfully than it is to pressurize yourself and your horse by attempting tests that are beyond your current capabilities.

As a general rule of thumb, you should wait until your scores are consistently above 65 percent before moving up to the next level. That way, you will ride down the centerline secure and confident in the knowledge that the level is well within your horse's comfort zone.

Tip #3. Learn your test!

Learn the test thoroughly! That sounds obvious, but it's amazing how many people enter the arena having just quickly looked over the test five minutes before their start time.

That's not to say that you should ride through the test endlessly at home, as doing so could lead to your horse anticipating the movements, which will lose you marks on the day. However, you do need to know where you're going so that you can prepare your horse for the next transition, half-pass, medium trot, etc.

If you're concerned that you might "go blank" on the day, ask someone to call the test for you so that you don't throw away marks by going wrong.

Tip #4. Read the directives

The test directives are shown on the dressage score sheet right next to the movements.

The directives are often used by the judge to justify their marks for that movement. For example, if you see that the judge has underlined "bend" or "lengthening of steps and frame," that immediately tells you where the marks for that movement were lost.

So, it's worth familiarizing yourself with the directives for each movement. For example, the directive for a serpentine mentions the equality of size of each loop. So, pay attention to the accuracy of your serpentine!

Tip #5. Visualize the test

A helpful tactic that will help you to remember the test is to visualize yourself riding it. That way, you can "ride" through the test as many times as you want to at home without the danger of your horse learning it too.

If you're familiar with the competition venue, it can be extremely helpful to visualize yourself riding a fabulous test in that arena. Once your subconscious mind has memorized that picture, it's much less likely that you'll forget your test on the day.

Tip #6. Please don't change!

Never make any changes right before a competition. That includes your way of riding and your equipment too.

For example, don't decide to wear spurs or use a double bridle if you don't generally use them at home. Even riding in new boots or a different jacket can affect your performance and upset your horse. If you feel stiff or uncomfortable, you won't be able to relax and ride to your best ability.

Finally, it's not a good idea to have a lesson with a new instructor right before a competition. That can leave you feeling confused and trying to change your riding too quickly. Wait until you have plenty of time to process your new coach's instruction and methods before you attempt to put them into practice in the arena.

Tip #7. Leave plenty of time to acclimatize at the venue

If you arrive late at the competition venue, you won't have time to look around and acclimatize yourself and your horse. Rushing can make you nervous, and that will be transmitted to your horse.

So, always set off in good time so that you'll have plenty of time to look around the event venue, watch a few tests, and go through your usual warm-up routine before you ride your test.

Riding the test

Most marks are thrown away during the actual riding of the test. Here are some simple tactics that can help you to maximize your scores every time!

Tip #8. Ride a good center line and halt

Many riders throw marks away right at the beginning of their test by not riding an accurate, straight center line and halt.

Make sure that you are right on the centerline, not to either side of it. Check the markers so that you ride the halt in the right place. If there is a judge at E or B, they will mark you down for halting early or late.

Practice riding a good halt at home so that you know you can replicate that in the arena. Don't always halt at X. Practice halting other places in the arena so that your horse doesn't anticipate always halting at X or G.

Also, make sure that you maintain the halt for a few seconds before moving off. Dressage test directives ask for "immobility" in the halt, so be sure to show it clearly.

Tip #9. Look where you're going!

It's incredible that so many riders ride the whole test with their gaze fixed firmly on their horse's plaits!

If you don't look up and look where you're going, you haven't a hope of being accurate. So, from the very first centerline, look ahead and prepare for the halt, turn at C, or whatever movement comes next.

Also, if you're riding a circle, looking up and around the circle means that your body is subtly positioned in such a way that you are giving your horse a clear turning aid.

Tip #10. Be accurate

Many marks are lost through inaccuracy.

Although demanding accuracy can sometimes seem petty, dressage tests are designed to show the judge that your horse is obedient to the aids and that you can, therefore, perform the movements precisely as directed.

So, don't throw marks away unnecessarily by carelessly riding circles that are too big, too small, or not centered at the prescribed marker. Make sure that serpentines have loops that are equal in size, and that transitions are ridden as your body passes the marker.

Tip #11. Keep focused if things go wrong

Everyone makes mistakes, even the greatest dressage riders.

If something goes wrong, put the error behind you and focus on what's coming up. Don't become a victim of "rabbit in headlights" syndrome; keep going!

Tip #12. Ride the walk properly

Many riders throw marks away by allowing their horse to drop behind the leg in the walk.

Remember that the mark awarded for the walk is often doubled.

Make sure that you keep the horse's attention and have him marching forward into the bridle, especially in the free walk. Don't forget to allow your horse plenty of rein in the free walk so that he can stretch, use his back, and cover the maximum amount of ground that his natural stride length allows.

Tip #13. Give and retake the reins clearly

If the test asks for a give and retake of the reins in trot or canter, make the release of the contact obvious to the judge!

The judge needs to clearly see that you have completely released the contact for a stride or two. All too often, the give and retake happens so quickly that it appears more like a nervous twitch! Blink, and you'll miss it!

Tip #14. Smile confidently!

No matter what happens during the test, smile and look confident right through to the bitter end!

In your final halt, look the judge in the eye, smile, and pat your horse. If you look defeated, cross and upset, that may be reflected in the judge's final marks.

Tip #15. Use the whole arena

When you ride your test, it's amazing how small the arena feels, especially if your horse is tense!

Make the most of every inch of space in the arena by riding deep into the corners, establishing good bend, and putting the horse well into your outside rein. Use that extra space to prepare your horse for every movement.

Tip #16. Check your position

Be sure to maintain your position when you're riding in a competition. Many riders get tense and nervous, so they tighten up. That can cause you to tip forward, look down, or become stiff through your shoulders and arms.

Remember that the mark for the rider includes "position" and "effectiveness." If you lose your position, you will become less effective, and that mark will be lower as a consequence.

Tip #17. Remember to count!

If the test asks you to halt for four seconds, make sure that you maintain the halt for the specified length of time. Many riders barely allow the horse to stop before walking on again, losing marks in the process!

Similarly, if you are asked to show three to five steps of rein-back, make sure that you don't show two or six!

Tip #18. Stick to your usual warm-up routine

Horses are more confident if they have a routine. That applies both to their daily yard routine and to their work.

When schooling your horse at home, work out a routine that makes your horse ready to perform a test, and use that same routine when you're warming-up at a competition.

Tip #19. Ride good transitions

Transitions, including half-halts, are an element of schooling that you will use dozens of times in every home-schooling session. So, when you ride a dressage test, don't neglect the transitions!

The judge will mark the transitions as part of a movement, so don't neglect that! Make your transitions balanced, round, and fluent, and you're sure to pick up extra marks right across the board.

Tip #20. Use psychology to help you keep your focus

When riding your test, imagine that you are wearing an earpiece through which your trainer is instructing you.

As you ride each movement, "hear" your trainer giving you directions.

For example, before each change of direction and transition, your instructor might tell you to ride a half-halt to rebalance your horse.

USING YOUR SCORESHEETS TO IMPROVE

Every time you ride in a dressage competition, you will receive a scoresheet at the conclusion of the class. Some people keep them simply for posterity if they are awarded especially good marks. Other riders keep sheets that they need to retain as qualification material for championships. But the most successful, savvy riders use their dressage scoresheets to improve their next performance, and you can do that too.

Test analysis

After every competition, take time out to analyze your dressage scoresheets in-depth to get the most benefit from them. Sit down with a cup of coffee and a notebook and go through your scoresheets with a fine-toothed comb. You're looking for anything that you can use to immediately improve your next test and devise a plan for long term goals.

Remember that dressage judges are highly trained and very experienced, usually as competition riders and trainers. So, their comments should be regarded as helpful and constructive, not merely as an excuse to deduct marks from competitors!

For your analysis exercise to be most effective, you'll need to use the scoresheets from your last two or three competitions. If you have video recordings of your tests, use those too. Watching the video and comparing your performance and scoresheets movement by movement can be a great way of seeing problems that you might not have been aware of before.

Understanding your dressage scoresheet

Before you can use your dressage scoresheet to improve your next performance, you must first understand how to interpret the sheet.

<u>Marks and comments</u>

First of all, it's very important that you don't get too hung up on the actual marks and the overall score that you receive for the test.

Here's why.

Essentially, the marks you're awarded for each individual movement will correlate to the comments that the judge makes. The marks that are awarded should reflect the definition given in the 'Scale of Marks' that's printed on the top of the scoresheet. For example, if the judge thinks that your 20-meter circle was quite nice, you'll most likely be given a mark of 7, which equates to "fairly good," according to the 'Scale of Marks'.

Judges are not required to make a comment unless they give a mark of 6 or below, and that can make it a tad tricky to interpret your sheet, especially when some judges' interpretation of the Scale is slightly at odds with others. In other words, what one judge might think is worth a mark of 7, someone else might only view as deserving of a 6.

Therefore, you can see right away that where one judge might award you 70%, a different judge may think that your performance was only worth 65% for exactly the same test, even though both judges' comments are remarkably similar.

So, although *points make prizes*, it's the judge's **comments** that are the most useful to you when using your dressage scoresheet to improve your future performance in the arena, rather than the score you were given.

Collective and overall comment

Of particular interest are the comments that appear alongside the 'Collective Marks' at the bottom of your scoresheet. The Collective Marks are awarded for paces, impulsion, submission, and for your riding position and the effectiveness of your aids.

The judge's comments in this section of the scoresheet relate to your horse's overall way of going and the way in which you rode and presented the test. You can use these comments to create a framework for future improvement in all these areas.

Understanding the judge's comments

Most riders who have been competing for any length of time will have a good understanding of the judge's comments that appear on their dressage scoresheets. However, if you're new to the sport, you might find a few of the often-used phrases are somewhat confusing. If this is you, we have a glossary of commonly used judges' remarks on our website. You can find it at howtodressage.com/competition/dressage-judges-comments

Step 1 – Quick wins and quick fixes

Before you analyze your scoresheet in-depth, begin by taking a quick look over the sheet to see if you threw away marks through making silly, unnecessary mistakes. Many marks are lost through a competitor's lack of understanding of the basic rules of the competition. So, before you rock-up at the event, make sure that you've read the rules from cover-to-cover first!

Here are a few common oversights that you can avoid next time:

- incorrect dress
- incorrect tack

- saluting incorrectly
- carrying a whip/wearing spurs when not permitted

<u>Wrong course!</u>

Another common slip-up that's made by a surprisingly high number of competitors is taking the wrong course.

Learn the test beforehand or have it called for you on the day, just in case you go wrong. Most event venues offer to provide competitors with a test caller in exchange for a small donation to a local charity, so you needn't worry about not having someone to call for you if you go to a competition on your own.

<u>Accuracy</u>

Look for comments relating to a lack of accuracy on your part. So, if you notice remarks such as, "circle too small," "circle not centered," "left of centerline," or "early to the track," then you know that you need to smarten up your act as far as being accurate is concerned.

Step 2 – Common denominators and long-term training

As you read through each scoresheet, you will most likely find a few common denominators.

For example, are you always marked down for not halting square? Perhaps every centerline you ride is left or right of center. Does your horse always hollow and rush during the medium trot, or does he drop behind your leg every time you ride a free walk?

Compare the comments that you receive for all the work on each rein. Do all your circles and turns on one rein lack bend while you have too much bend on the opposite rein? Does the judge always remark that you are leaning to one side or continually looking down?

These are all clues to fundamental factors in your horse's way of going and your own riding that should be addressed during your daily schooling sessions.

Make a list of everything that's highlighted more than once and use your notes to create a training plan that will gradually improve your overall performance.

It's also extremely helpful to go through the list you've made with your trainer, who will then be equipped to help you in devising an ongoing training regimen that will address the points raised.

Tortoise and hare

You will now have two sets of notes or lists. One set will contain "quick wins" that you can address right away. The other list will contain observations on the horse's basic way of going that will take more time and systematic training to improve.

Competition level

Something that will quickly become evident when studying your scoresheets is whether you are over facing your horse with the level at which you are competing.

A good way of checking that is by comparing the comments with the basic Dressage Scales of Training. The Scales apply to every level of competition and must be securely in place before you move from one level to the next. For example, if you are competing at elementary level and you are continually being given comments such as "lacking bend" or "circle too big" on the smaller circles that are demanded in the test, it's likely that your horse is not yet sufficiently submissive and supple to the bend to be able to perform the movements adequately at that level, especially if those remarks are accompanied by "on the forehand!" In that case, it may be advisable to step back a level in competition while you are working on developing the horse's lateral suppleness.

Next steps

Each time you compete, read through your scoresheets and compare them with the lists you made. All the "quick fix" items on your list should be gone!

Gradually, you will see some of the comments that kept cropping up that related to the horse's way of going begin to disappear, as your revised training program takes effect, and your horse progresses in his schooling.

Don't panic if you start to see different comments appearing on your scoresheets! That's to be expected as you and your horse progress up the grades. All you need to do is apply the same analysis technique as before and use your findings to take your performance to the next level.

Dressage Performance Analysis Workbook

Here at How To Dressage, we created a workbook specifically designed to help you analyze your dressage scores.

To find out more about it, check out our Facebook Page or search Amazon for "Dressage Performance Analysis by HowToDressage".

WHEN TO MOVE UP TO THE NEXT LEVEL

When beginning your dressage career with your ex-racehorse, I'm sure you'll be eager to progress up the levels with him.

You can use the dressage test series as a framework within which to train your horse. However, a few tests with poor marks can leave you feeling discouraged and you may not want to move up a level until you have 'perfected' everything and you're regularly scoring 8's and 9's. This can leave you remaining in the lower levels for what feels like forever.

So, how do you gauge when it's time to move your horse up to the next level in competition?

Here are some pointers to help you make our own decision as to when the time might be right to move on to the next level in your horse's training.

When should you move your horse up to the next level in his training?

Start by reading ALL the tests at the next level up to get a good idea of the movements and questions that are required of your horse.

Remember, all the movements sound easy when written on paper! So, train yourself to visualize how you and your horse would look at the next level up. Analyze what you would find straightforward and what you would find difficult.

Analyze how your horse feels

Analyzing how your horse feels is the main barometer of knowing when to upgrade to the next level.

- Is he fitter and stronger? A correct way of going develops physical and mental strength and coordination.
- Does he recover quickly after cantering on the right rein, then the left rein?
- Are the transitions balanced and seamless?
- Do the transitions happen mainly from your seat, and with positively received leg and rein aids to assist?

Analyze the quality of the transitions

Firstly, they should be prompt off the aids. Then the horse should stay forwards, whilst accepting the contact.

You should feel more and more of his balance coming onto the hindquarters which means that less and less weight and resistance is loaded onto the horse's shoulders, head, mouth, and consequently your hands, arms, and shoulders, enabling you to say stronger through your core.

Onlookers will let you know about your improvement. Somebody who has not seen your horse work for a month or two will notice big improvement just after working through easy and direct transitions.

Analyze the movements

Try individual movements in tests at the next level up and analyze how they feel.

The committees who design the tests intend to put transitions, 10-meter circles, and rein backs in front of the judge at 'C'! So, if your horse is not balanced on the hindquarters, or tilts his head, or struggles to step back in diagonal pairs on the bit in rein back, then accept that the marks will be low, or adapt your training sessions to improve these areas.

Ride through the test

When you feel the time is right to try the next level, ride through the test calmly at home.

At first, when riding a test at the next level above, movements will seem to come up very quickly. When you feel as if you have 'time' to think of how you should present your horse through the test and not just where to go between the markers, you probably have enough control to try the test competitively.

How to know when your horse is NOT ready for the next level

Do not enter a test at a new level without reading through it first many days beforehand. This will give you time to feel if you and your horse are ready to cope together.

Many riders try a new level without any preparation and rarely is the presentation good. From a judge's perspective, it usually looks rough and more often than not both horse and rider appear overloaded.

Do not underestimate the location and placement of the transitions in the test, particularly in the canter. They will come to you quickly in the test and this is where you need to know you have time to balance your horse. If you don't have time to balance your horse, you will make mistakes, and one mistake quickly leads to another.

Do not forget to ride the horse in the test exactly as you do at home. He must receive the same instructions and aids, and then you will realize that you can trust him. When you can trust and rely on him, you will both be more confident, and this brings higher marks.

Notes about moving up a level

It can be tempting to rush ahead with your horse's training; after all, no-one wants to be a 'novice' forever. However, it is important for your own confidence, and that of your horse, not to rush things. Know that you can easily perform all the requirements for the level in your training at home before entering a test at that level.

Don't be too disheartened if your first few tests at the new level receive lower marks than you usually get at your current level. Remember that the judge will be expecting more engagement, uphill carriage, and suppleness as the levels progress, as well as looking to see that your horse can perform all the actual movements required.

BONUS SECTION:
JUMPING

HOW TO START JUMPING YOUR EX-RACEHORSE

Although this book is primarily about transforming your ex-racehorse into a dressage superstar, some of you reading this may also want to jump your horse. Therefore, we have added this bonus section to help you get going.

Before you begin jump training, it's important that you have a solid dressage foundation. If you start jumping your ex-racer too soon, you risk pushing your horse's weight onto his forehand and causing him to 'run' as he tries to find his balance.

For safety reasons, you should always have an assistant with you when you're schooling over fences; even if you are just riding over poles on the ground, the horse can easily trip.

If this is your first time introducing a horse to jumping, we recommend that you work with an experienced trainer. Mistakes at this stage can be very costly. At worst, you and your horse could be injured, and you could also hinder any progress you've made by giving your horse a scare. Providing your horse with a positive first experience is crucial to his success, so if you are at all in doubt, always ask an experienced friend or professional for help.

Also, we suggest that you ride your ex-racer in his usual snaffle bit and running martingale. If the horse is correctly schooled on the flat, you shouldn't need to use anything stronger in your horse's mouth, and the martingale helps to prevent the horse from bringing his head up beyond the point of control. The martingale also doubles-up as a neck strap. Inexperienced horses have a tendency to overjump, and you can put your fingers under the neck strap if you need to, rather than catching your horse in the mouth.

Jumping technique

As far as jumping technique goes, a jump is nothing more than an exaggerated canter stride. Ideally, the horse should "bascule" over the fence, arching his back, lifting his forehand, and throwing his hind legs up and clear of the pole. If your ex-racer comes from a steeplechasing or hurdling background, he will naturally jump out of his stride, but he will flatten instead of basculing. That's because jump racers are trained to get from one side of the fence to the other as quickly as possible, brushing through the top of a birch fence or kicking the top of a hurdle.

That's where your dressage work comes in! Your horse has learned to work through a supple back and neck into the contact in a round frame, which is what you want him to do when he's jumping. When the horse bascules over a fence, it's much less likely that he will take a pole with him than if he jumps flat with his hind legs trailing.

There are five phases of a jump:

1. Approach
2. Take-off
3. Flight
4. Landing
5. Getaway

Remember that you're aiming for a bascule shape throughout the jump.

Ground poles

For your horse's first lesson, always start with a single pole on the ground. If you've already used poles as part of your flatwork schooling, that shouldn't faze your horse. However, if not, it's highly likely that this will be the first time your ex-racer has ever seen a pole.

So, start on the ground by leading your horse over the pole in a walk. It's sensible to have a helper on the other side of the horse too to give your ex-racer extra confidence. Leading the horse will give you an idea of what could happen when you get on board. If the horse reluctant, recruit a calm, experienced horse to act as a "buddy" for your ex-racer to follow. At this stage, once your horse is relaxed, it's also a good idea to place two wings on either side of the pole. If the horse tends to wander or lose straightness on the approach to the pole, place two poles parallel to each other as a guide on approach and after the poles.

Once the horse is relaxed and walking calmly over the pole from both directions, you can ride him over it. If you need to follow a "buddy" horse or have someone walk alongside your ex-racer, then do so. It's better to give your horse an enjoyable, stress-free experience than to frighten him. If all goes well, try trotting over the pole.

Now, you can put out two more poles at a suitable trot stride distance apart. Take things slowly, as it may take your horse a few tries to figure out where his feet should go! So, be ready to grab your neck strap, and don't tip too far forward in case your horse trips. Allow the horse to stretch his neck down so that he can see where he's putting his feet. Once the horse can negotiate three poles successfully, you can up the ante by introducing two more poles.

When riding over poles, always keep your weight in your heels, look up, and be prepared in case the horse stag-jumps the poles. Be ready to give the rein and go with the horse so that you don't accidentally jab him in the mouth or offer him any negative pressure.

Focus on keeping the horse straight and in a steady, relaxed rhythm. Give your horse plenty of encouragement with your voice and by patting him down the neck, and keep every session simple, short, and sweet.

First fences

Once the horse is confident with trotting over poles on the ground, you can introduce a small fence. To begin with, set up a tiny cross-pole. Begin by approaching in trot in the same way as you approached the poles, riding down your "tramlines" of parallel poles, and aiming for the lowest part of the cross-pole.

At this stage, approach the fence in trot. Approaching in canter means that everything happens too fast at this early stage in your horse's training, and trotting into the jump keeps everything simpler for you as a rider too.

Don't worry about trying to pick a takeoff spot; the horse will soon work that out for himself. Just ride forward in a steady rhythm and be prepared for a huge leap! Keep your hands soft and forward, be ready to grab the neck strap, and keep your weight into your heels and be ready to go with the horse when he jumps, rather than being left behind.

When your horse can confidently pop over the cross-pole, put the fence up to a straight bar.

If your horse begins to get excited and anticipates jumping the fence, work around it too, riding in a circle. Approaching the fence from an arc helps to keep the horse relaxed and in a steady tempo and rhythm and prevents him from rushing at the jump. If the horse tries to charge into the fence, circle away, re-establish the tempo and rhythm, and re-present the horse at the fence.

Cantering into fences

When the horse is jumping confidently from trot, you can begin cantering into the fence. To give the horse an idea of where to take off, you can use a ground pole appropriately placed in front of the fence.

Remember that a jump is simply an exaggerated canter stride. So, don't be tempted to start fussing with the horse's stride as you approach the jump. Instead, maintain a calm, steady rhythm and tempo, keep the horse straight, and aim for the center of the fence. The canter tempo and rhythm should remain the same during the approach, the jump, and the getaway.

Introducing fillers

Fillers should only be introduced when the horse is confidently jumping colored poles.

Begin by using a simple natural brush filler (rather than anything too crazy), placing two fillers at angles slightly in front of the pole so that there is a gap between them for the horse to focus on.

Once the horse is jumping that confidently, gradually, decrease the gap until the fillers are underneath the fence.

Connecting fences

Once the horse is confidently jumping colored poles and a few fillers, you can start connecting fences in a small course.

To begin with, keep the fences very small and simple to build confidence. You can introduce related distances, combinations, doubles, dog-legs, and more complex lines when the horse is more experienced.

Height of fences

Keep the fences small to build your horse's confidence. In the beginning, you are training for rhythm and technique, not for height. If you make the fences too big before your horse is confident and ready for the challenge, you risk destroying all your hard work and ending up back where you started.

Also, novice jumpers tend to cat-leap or overjump, which can leave you behind or even jumped-off altogether. If you keep the jumps small, the horse is less likely to put in a leap that unseats you.

Troubleshooting

As the horse gathers experience and grows more confident, you shouldn't have many problems. However, there are a few stumbling blocks that you may encounter which are especially common in ex-racers.

Overjumping

Many horses overjump when they first start jumping, and that can happen over ground poles too. Be ready for your horse to take a huge leap and try to relax. Once the horse realizes that he doesn't need to put in quite so much effort, the overjumping habit will disappear.

Nerves

Being nervous when you begin training your ex-racer for jumping is nothing to be ashamed of! Try to stay relaxed and keep your leg on positively. Use your voice to encourage your horse, too, but let him work it out himself, and don't worry if he knocks the fences down, that's all part of the learning process.

Racing away

A super-quick getaway on landing after a fence is not uncommon in ex-racers, especially ex-jumpers, as that's what they have been trained to do. Focus on regaining the same tempo and rhythm that you had on your approach to the jump as quickly as possible. However, remember that shortening the reins can encourage a racehorse to go faster, so try slipping your reins slightly instead as you land.

As with every element of your ex-racer's re-training program, you must be ready to go back a step or two if things go wrong.

WHAT NEXT?

Finished?

We really hope that you have found this book helpful when buying, re-training, and competing your off-the-track thoroughbred in dressage.

Here's what to do next.

The OTTB community

Check out social media and you'll discover various groups of people who own ex-racehorses. These are great communities for you to join and become part of.

Most of the national ex-racer rescues have forums too where you can exchange tips and success stories with other people who have grown to know and love these beautiful horses and who have given these highborn equine athletes a second chance.

Check out our other books

We have a whole range of books, training diaries, and workbooks available on Amazon to help you progress even further with your training.

To view them all, simply search for 'How To Dressage' on Amazon or drop by our Facebook Page.

Keep an eye on our website

Dressage training is never-ending – and so is our website!

New articles are being published every week on HowToDressage.com. To help make sure that you don't miss any, remember to subscribe to our mailing list and follow our Facebook Page.

Visit our forum

We've recently launched a new dressage training forum on our website, and we'd love for you to pop by.

As with all forums, there's a place for discussing everything that is dressage, competitions and horse care. But we also welcome equestrian bloggers and business and encourage them to share their websites, blog posts, products, sales and discounts.

You can join free at **HowToDressage.com/Community**

Ask us your questions

Do you have any other questions that we didn't answer in this book? No problem!

Send your question to hello@howtodressage.com and we will gladly get one of our dressage judges to answer it for you in a future post on our website – it may even end up in one of our next books!

Leave a review

We would love to know what you thought of this book.

If you can spare a few minutes, please head over to Amazon and leave us an honest review.

If you have any feedback that you would like to share with us directly, please email hello@howtodressage.com

Free stuff!

We have a whole range of free stuff available on our website, including free downloads and free email courses.

To check them all out, just go to – **HowToDressage.com/free-stuff**

Share your photos

We love to see our books getting put to good use so please share your photos on social media using the hashtag **#RacehorseToDressageHorse** - and don't forget to tag us!

Finally…

Re-training an ex-racehorse is no small task. It takes a lot of time and a lot of patience.

You will most likely experience some sticking points where things may get a little frustrating. In these times, remember to look back on your progress and take pride in how far you have both come.

You have given a horse a second-chance and a new career, and that is worth far more than any rosette.

How To Dressage xx

Printed in Great Britain
by Amazon